KU-492-813

Chambers
Phrasal
Verbs

Chambers
Phrasal Verbs

Edited by

George W. Davidson

Chambers

CHAMBERS
An imprint of Larousse plc
43–45 Annandale Street
Edinburgh EH7 4AZ

Original from
Chambers Universal Learners' Dictionary
Copyright © Larousse plc

First published 1982 as
Times-Chambers *Dictionary of Phrasal Verbs*
by Federal Publications (S) Pte Ltd
by arrangement with W & R Chambers

Reprinted 1984, 1986, 1987 (twice), 1989
          1990, 1991, 1993 (twice), 1994

© 1982 Federal Publications (S) Pte Ltd
A member of the Times Publishing Group
Times Centre
1 New Industrial Road
Singapore 1953

ISBN 0-550-18030-3

Printed and bound in Great Britain by Cox & Wyman Ltd

Preface

Learning English presents difficulties both for those whose mother tongue it is and for those who learn it as a foreign language. The nature of these difficulties, as well as the scale of them, however, is different for each of these categories of learner. This is particularly true of phrasal verbs. The ability to use phrasal verbs correctly is almost instinctive in the native speaker, but non-native learners of English often find great difficulty in mastering the various meanings and constructions of such verbs.

It is important for non-native learners to learn how to use phrasal verbs correctly for they are very much used in everyday speech and in idiomatic expressions. Obviously learners of English as a foreign language must have mastered basic English vocabulary and grammar before tackling phrasal verbs. They will thus be at an intermediate stage of learning English.

Phrasal verbs consist of simple verbs such as **make, get, go, look, sit,** together with adverbs or prepositions, *eg* **on, up, out.** Although these look like phrases in that they are composed of more than one word, they often function like a single word, and frequently have a meaning not deducible from the literal meanings of the verb and the particle(s) of which the phrasal verb is composed, *eg* **put up with.**

Headwords and labels

The phrasal verbs in this dictionary are listed in alphabetical order. Each entry consists of a headword — the phrasal verb — in bold type followed by the grammatical label, *eg vt fus* or *vt sep* in italic type, followed by the definition in roman type, followed by an example in italics of how to use the phrase.

For reasons of space and convenience some phrasal verbs have been treated together in a single entry. Thus **aim to** and **aim at** appear as **aim to/at**. Differences in constructions are reflected in the examples.

Where a particular phrasal verb has more than one meaning the definitions have been clearly numbered to avoid confusion. Some phrasal verbs have a label, placed after the grammatical label, to indicate the context or situation in which they are usually used. For example, all the definitions of **buck up** are labelled (*inf*) since they commonly occur where the user is speaking or writing in an informal situation or context.

> **buck up 1** *vi* (*inf*) to hurry: *You'd better buck up if you want to catch the bus.* **2** *vi, vt sep* (*inf*) to cheer up: *The good news will buck her up. She bucked up when she heard the news.* **3** *vi, vt sep* (*inf*) to improve (one's attitude *etc*): *Buck up your ideas or you'll be out of a job.*

Similarly **allude to** has been labelled (*formal*) since it is commonly used only in formal contexts, and **go forth** has been labelled (*arch or liter*) since, although not common in modern English, it appears in archaic or literary English.

Sometimes opinions vary as to what constitutes a phrasal verb. In this dictionary constructions such as **apply for** have been labelled as phrasal verbs, and any words which may separate the verb from the preposition in such cases have been put in brackets, *eg You could apply (to the manager) for a job.*

Classification of verbs

One of the major problems which the non-native learner of English encounters when attempting to master phrasal verb constructions is knowing whether or not a particular phrasal verb can take an object, and if so, where to place the object in relation to the simple verb and the particle(s) of which the phrasal verb is composed. To assist the learner with this problem, all phrasal verbs have been labelled as transitive or intransitive in the way that verbs are usually classified in dictionaries.

Phrasal verbs labelled *vi* are phrases which function like intransitive verbs and so do not take a direct object.

> **get about** *vi* **1** (of stories, rumours *etc*) to become well known: *I don't know how the story got about that she was leaving.* **2** to be able to move or travel about, often of people who have been ill: *She didn't get about much after her operation. Now that they have sold their car, they don't get about a lot.*

Phrasal verbs labelled *vt* are phrases which function like transitive verbs and so can take a direct object. Transitive phrasal verbs are further classified into *vt sep* — separable transitive verbs — or *vt fus* — fused transitive verbs. A separable phrasal verb, labelled *vt sep*, is one in which the words — *ie* the verb and adverb — that go together to make up the phrase <u>may</u> be separated from each other by the object where the object is a noun. Alternatively the object, if it is a noun, may be placed after the accompanying adverb. Thus it is permissible to say *She put aside her work* or *She put her work aside*.

If the object of a separable phrasal verb is not a noun but a pronoun, it must come between the verb and the adverb. This means that if you wish to use 'it' instead of 'her work' in the above example, then the sentence becomes *She put it aside* and not *She put aside it*.

A transitive phrasal verb which is obligatorily separated, labelled *vt oblig sep*, is one in which the object, whether it is a noun or a pronoun, must separate the verb from the adverb, as in **push around** meaning 'to treat roughly'. For example, *He pushes his young brother around* is the correct form for this sense of the verb.

A transitive phrasal verb which is usually separated, labelled *vt usually sep*, is one in which the object, if a noun, <u>usually</u> separates the verb from the adverb. Of course, where the object is a pronoun, it <u>always</u> separates the verb from the particle.

A fused transitive phrasal verb, labelled *vt fus*, is one in which the words that go together to make up the phrase are 'fused' together. In other words, the verb <u>cannot</u> be separated from the accompanying preposition by the object, whether it is a noun or a pronoun. For example, all four meanings of the phrasal verb **go with** in the following example are labelled *vt fus* because you cannot separate **go** from **with** by an object.

> **go with** *vt fus* **1** to be given or sold with (something): *The carpets will go with the house.* **2** to look, taste *etc* well with (something): *The carpet goes with the wallpaper. Whisky doesn't go very well with tea.* **3** to be found in the same place as (something): *Illness often goes with poverty.* **4** to go steady with (someone): *I've been going with Mary for six months.*

Note that an adverb or an adverbial phrase describing the verb may separate the verb and the preposition although the object may not separate them, *eg Whisky doesn't go very well with tea.*

Some fused transitive phrasal verbs are made up of more than two words, *eg* **put up with**. In this case the phrasal verb is made up of the verb **put**, the adverb **up**, and the preposition **with**. In phrasal verbs of this kind the adverb and the preposition may not be separated from each other by the object and they may not be separated from the verb by the object. For example, it is correct to say *I cannot put up with all this noise,* but incorrect to say *I cannot put up all this noise with* or *I cannot put all this noise up with.*

Position of labels

The labels are arranged in such a way to give specific information that will help learners to use the phrasal verbs correctly and in the right context. If a label applies to all of the meanings of a phrasal verb, the label comes before the numbering sequence begins, *ie* before the number 1:

> **catch on** *vi* (*inf*) **1** to become popular. **2** to understand.

This indicates that both meanings of **catch on** are intransitive verbs and are informal.

If the label is placed immediately after one of the numbers in a definition, it indicates that the label applies only to the meaning immediately following:

> **get off 1** *vi, vt fus* to leave (a bus, train *etc*). **2** *vi* (*inf*) to leave (a place).

This indicates that the first meaning of **get off** is both an intransitive verb and a fused transitive verb, and the second meaning is an intransitive verb and is informal.

If there is a label after one of the numbers in a definition and there is also a label which comes before the whole numbering sequence, then both labels apply to the definition so labelled:

> **get at** *vt fus* **1** to reach (a place, thing *etc*). **2** (*inf*) to suggest or imply (something). **3** (*inf*) to point out (a person's faults) or make fun of (a person).

This indicates that all the meanings of **get at** are fused transitive verbs, and only the second and third meanings are informal.

Definitions

For reasons of space the literal meanings of phrasal verbs have not usually been given in this dictionary. Thus the phrasal verb **get across** is given in its figurative sense, but not in the literal sense of *He got across the river* (= He succeeded in crossing the river).

> **get across** *vi, vt usually sep* (*inf*) to be or make (something) understood: *This is something which rarely gets across to the general public. The plan seems quite clear to me, but I just can't get it across (to anyone else).*

Similarly the phrasal verb **get into** is given in its figurative senses, but not in its literal sense as used in *Please go into the room.*

> **go into** *vt fus* **1** to make a careful study (of something): *We'll need to go into this plan in more detail before we make any decision.* **2** to discuss or describe (something) in detail: *I don't want to go into the problems at the moment as there isn't any time before my next appointment.* **3** to begin to do (something) as a job: *My son hopes to go into politics.*

Learners wishing more information on the literal meanings of verbs, adverbs and prepositions will find these fully dealt with in **Chambers Universal Learners' Dictionary.**

Verb phrases

A few verb phrases consisting of verb plus object followed by preposition plus object have been listed in the dictionary (although they are not usually regarded as phrasal verbs) because it was felt that they would be useful for learners. They have been labelled simply as *vt* as in **apply to:** *apply force to a door* — and **build on** (definition 3): *I've built all my hopes on this book being published.* More verb constructions of this type can be found in **Chambers Universal Learners' Dictionary.**

This dictionary with its numerous examples showing how phrasal verbs are actually used will be invaluable to learners of English as a foreign language. It will not only help them to understand phrasal verbs but will give them the knowledge and confidence to use them.

Labels used in this Dictionary

Amer	American
arch	archaic
derog	derogatory
euph	euphemistic
facet	facetious
fig	figurative
formal	—
inf	informal
legal	—
liter	literary
mil	military
neg	negative
old	—
passive	—
sl	slang
v refl	reflexive verb
vt	verb transitive
vt fus	verb transitive fused
vt oblig sep	verb transitive obligatorily separated
vt sep	verb transitive separable
vt usually sep	verb transitive usually separated
vulg	vulgar

A

abide by *vt fus* to act according to; to be faithful to: *They must abide by the rules of the game.*

abstain from *vt fus* not to do, take *etc* (something): *He abstained from voting in the election. (formal) He abstained from alcohol.*

accede to *vt fus (formal)* to agree to: *He acceded to my request.*

account for *vt fus* **1** to give a reason for; to explain: *I can account for the mistake.* **2** *(formal)* to settle or deal with successfully: *The army accounted for large numbers of the enemy.*

act as *vt fus* to do the work or duties of: *He acts as head of department when his boss is away. This sofa also acts as a bed.*

act for *vt fus* to do something for (someone else); to act as the representative of (someone): *She is acting for the headmaster in his absence.*

act on / *(formal)* **upon** *vt fus* **1** to do something following (the advice, instructions *etc* of someone): *I am acting on the advice of my lawyer. Have you acted on his instructions/suggestions?* **2** to have an effect on: *Certain acids act on metal.*

act up *vi (inf)* to behave or act badly or wrongly: *That child always acts up when his father is away. My car always acts up on a long journey. My injured leg is acting up again.*

add to *vt fus* to increase: *The news added to our happiness. His illness had added to their difficulties.*

add together / **up** *vt sep* to add and find the total of: *Add these figures together. He added up the column of figures.*

1

add up

add up *vi (inf)* to seem sensible or logical: *I don't understand his behaviour — it just doesn't add up.*

adhere to *vt fus* **1** *(formal)* to stick to: *This tape doesn't adhere to the floor very well.* **2** to remain loyal to: *I'm adhering to my principles.*

adjust to *vt fus* to change in order to become more suitable for or adapted to: *He soon adjusted to his new way of life.*

agree on/ *(formal)* **upon** *vt fus* **1** to discuss and come to the same decision about: *We agreed on a date for our next holiday.* **2** to have the same opinion as someone else about: *We may belong to different political parties, but there are some things we agree on.*

agree to *vt fus* to say that one will do or allow something: *He agreed to our request.*

agree with *vt fus* **1** to think or say the same as: *I agreed with them that we should try again.* **2** to be good for the health *etc* of: *Cheese does not agree with me.* **3** *(grammar)* to be in the same tense, case, person *etc* as: *The verb must agree with its subject.*

aim at/for *vt fus* to point or direct something at; to try to hit or reach *etc: He aimed a blow at her head. (fig) He is aiming for the top of his profession.*

aim to/at *vt fus* to plan or intend: *He aims to finish the book next week. He aims at finishing the job tomorrow.*

alight on/ *(formal)* **upon** *vt fus* to settle or land on: *The bird alighted on the fence. (fig) His eyes alighted on the letter.*

allow for *vt fus* to take into consideration when judging or deciding (especially a future possibility): *These figures allow for price rises. We must allow for an emergency.*

allude to *vt fus (formal)* to speak of indirectly or mention in passing: *He did not allude to the remarks made by the previous speaker.*

answer for *vt fus* **1** to bear the responsibility or be responsible for (something): *I'll answer (to your mother) for your safety.* **2** to suffer or be punished for (something): *You'll answer for your rudeness one day.*

answer to *vt fus* to be the same as or correspond to (a description *etc*): *The police have found a man answering to that description.*

apply for *vt fus* to ask for (something) formally: *You could apply (to the manager) for a job. He applied for financial help.*

apply to 1 *vt* to use (something) for (some purpose): *to apply force to a door that will not open. He applied his knowledge of the country to planning their escape.* **2** *vt fus* to concern or be relevant to: *This rule does not apply to him.* **3** *vt fus* to ask for something formally from: *If you want a loan from the bank, you have to apply to the manager in writing.*

approve of *vt fus* to be pleased with or think well of (a person *etc*): *I approve of your decision.*

argue for/against *vt fus* (*formal*) to suggest reasons for or for not (doing something): *I argued for accepting the plan. He argued against Britain joining the EEC.*

arrive at *vt fus* to reach (a place *etc*): *We arrived at the station as the train was leaving.* (*fig*) *The committee failed to arrive at a decision.* (*fig*) *We both arrived at the same conclusion.*

ask after *vt fus* to make inquiries about the state of: *She asked after his father.*

ask for *vt fus* **1** to express a wish to see or speak to (someone): *When he telephoned he asked for you. He is very ill and keeps asking for his daughter.* **2** to behave as if inviting (something unpleasant): *Going out in cold weather without a coat is just asking for trouble. She asked for all she got.*

aspire to *vt fus* (*formal*) to try very hard to reach (something difficult, ambitious *etc*): *He aspired to the position of president.*

attend to *vt fus* to listen or give attention to: *Attend carefully to what the lecturer is saying!*

average out *vt sep* to work out the average result: *He averaged out his expenses at ten dollars per day. He averaged them out.*

average out at *vt fus* to result in as an average: *His car's petrol consumption averaged out at ten litres a week.*

B

back down *vi* to give up one's opinion, claim, *etc*: *She backed down in the face of strong opposition.*

back out 1 *vi, vt sep* to move out backwards: *He opened the garage door and backed (his car) out.* **2** *vi* to withdraw from a promise *etc*: *You promised to help — you mustn't back out now!*

back up *vt sep* to support or encourage: *The new evidence backed up my arguments. Her husband never seems to back her up.*

bail out *vt sep* to set (a person) free by giving money to a court of law: *They won't allow you to bail out someone accused of murder.*

bale out 1 *vi* to parachute from a plane in an emergency. **2** *vi, vt sep* to clear water out of a boat: *We shall have to bale (the water/boat) out.*

bank on *vt fus (inf)* to rely on: *I'm banking on his help to run the disco. Don't bank on me — I'll probably be late.*

bargain for *vt fus (often in neg)* to expect or take into consideration: *I didn't bargain for everyone arriving at once. He got much more than he bargained for when he started arguing with her.*

bash in *vt sep (inf)* to beat or smash: *The soldiers bashed in the door.*

bash on *vi (sl)* to go on doing something especially in a careless or inattentive way: *In spite of his father's advice he bashed on (with the painting).*

bear out *vt sep (formal)* to support or confirm: *This bears out what you said. If you put in a complaint about him, I will bear you out.*

bear with *vt fus (formal)* to be patient with (someone):

Bear with me for a minute, and you'll see what I mean.

beat down 1 *vi* (of the sun) to give out great heat: *The sun's rays beat down on us in the desert.* **2** *vt sep* to reduce (the price of something) by bargaining: *We managed to beat the price down by $5.* **3** *vt sep* to force (a person) to lower a price: *We tried to beat him down but we had to pay the full price in the end.*

beat off *vt sep* to succeed in overcoming or preventing: *The old man beat off the youths who attacked him. He beat the attack off easily.*

beat up *vt sep* to punch, kick or hit (a person) severely and repeatedly: *They beat my brother up and left him for dead. He beat up an old lady.*

believe in *vt fus* **1** to accept the existence of (something) as a fact: *Do you believe in ghosts?* **2** to recognize the value or advantage of (something): *Some doctors believe in a low-fat diet. He believes in capital punishment.* **3** to have faith in the ability *etc* of (someone): *He will achieve his ambition — he really believes in himself.*

belong in *vt fus* to have as its correct place: *These shoes belong in the cupboard.*

belong to *vt fus* **1** to be the property of: *The book belongs to me. The furniture belongs to my mother.* **2** to be a native, member *etc* of: *I belong to Glasgow. Singapore belongs to the ASEAN.*

belong with *vt fus* to go along or together with: *This page belongs with all the others. This shoe belongs with that shoe.*

bestow on/upon *vt* (formal) to give (especially a title, award *etc*) to (someone): *The Queen bestowed a knighthood on him.*

beware of *vt fus* to be careful of: *Beware of the dog. Beware of thieves.*

blare out *vi*, *vt sep* to sound loudly and often harshly: *The radio was blaring out (pop music) constantly.*

blast off *vi* (of rockets, spacecraft *etc*) to take off and start to rise.

blast out *vi*, *vt sep* to come or be sent out, very loudly: *Music (was being) blasted out from the radio.*

blot out *vt sep* **1** to hide from sight: *The rain blotted out the view.* **2** to conceal or remove from memory: *I've blotted out all memory of that terrible day.*

blow out *vt sep* to extinguish or put out (a flame *etc*) by blowing: *The wind blew out the candle. The child blew out the match.*

blow up **1** *vi*, *vt sep* to break into pieces, or be broken into pieces, by an explosion: *The bridge blew up. The soldiers blew the factory up.* **2** *vt sep* to fill with air or a gas: *He blew up the balloon. He blew the tyre up with difficulty.* **3** *vi (inf)* to lose one's temper: *If he says that again I'll blow up.* **4** *vt sep* to enlarge (a photograph *etc*). **5** *vt sep (sl)* to scold or speak to (someone) angrily: *She blew me up for arriving late.*

blurt out *vt sep* to say (something) suddenly or without thinking of the effect or result: *He blurted out the whole story.*

book in **1** *vi* to sign one's name on the list of guests at a hotel *etc*: *We have booked in at the Royal Hotel.* **2** *vt sep* to reserve a place for (someone) in a hotel *etc*: *My aunt is coming to stay so I've booked her in at the nearest hotel.*

boom out *vi* to make a hollow sound, like a large drum or gun: *His voice boomed out over the loudspeaker.*

bottle up *vt sep* to prevent (*eg* one's feelings) from becoming known or obvious: *Don't bottle up your anger — tell him what's annoying you.*

break away *vi* to escape from control: *The dog broke away from its owner.* (*fig*) *Several of the states broke away and became independent.*

break down **1** *vt sep* to use force on (a door *etc*) to cause it to open, sometimes resulting in breaking it: *We had to break the door down because we lost the key.* **2** *vi* to stop working properly: *My car has broken down.* **3** *vi* to fail; to be unsuccessful and so come to an end: *The talks have broken down.* **4** *vi* to be overcome with emotion: *She broke down and wept.* **5** *vt sep* to divide into parts: *The results can be broken down in several ways. The chemist has broken the compound down into its parts.*

break in(to) *vi, vt fus* **1** to enter (a house *etc*) by force or unexpectedly: *When the burglar broke in he was bitten by my dog. Someone tried to break into the house.* **2** to interrupt (someone's conversation *etc*): *He broke in with a rude remark. He broke into our conversation.*

break into *vt fus* to begin (something) suddenly: *He broke into song* (= began singing). *His face broke into a smile.*

break off *vi, vt sep* **1** to stop: *He broke off communications with his family. She broke off in the middle of a sentence. They broke the engagement off yesterday.* **2** to (cause to) come off by breaking: *I've broken the handle off. The handle has broken off.*

break out *vi* **1** to appear or happen suddenly: *War has broken out.* **2** to escape (from prison, restrictions *etc*): *A prisoner has broken out.* **3** to become suddenly covered (in a rash *etc*): *Her face has broken out in a rash.*

break up 1 *vi, vt sep* to divide or break into pieces: *The sheet of ice is breaking up. He broke the old furniture up and sold the wood. (fig) The policeman broke up the crowd. (fig) John and Mary broke up* (= separated from each other) *last week. (fig) Their marriage has broken up.* **2** *vi* to finish or end: *The meeting broke up at 4.40. The schools break up for the holidays soon.*

break with *vt fus* **1** to quarrel with and therefore stop being connected with: *He broke with the Labour Party in 1968. He broke with it some time ago.* **2** to depart from; to cease to follow: *He broke with tradition and married a girl of a different race.*

breathe in, out 1 *vi* to cause air to enter or leave the lungs by breathing: *He couldn't breathe in until he reached the surface.* **2** *vt sep* to cause (a gas, particles of dust *etc*) to enter or leave the lungs by breathing: *The workers had breathed in large quantities of poison gas.*

brick up *vt sep* **1** to close (a hole *etc*) with bricks: *They*

bricked up the fireplace. They bricked it up yesterday.
2 to imprison (a person) behind a wall of bricks: *She was bricked up alive and died a horrible death.*

brim over *vi* to overflow: *The cup is brimming over with water. (fig) She is brimming over with excitement.*

bring about *vt sep* to cause: *His disregard for danger brought about his death. What brought it about?*

bring back *vt sep* to (cause to) return: *May I borrow your pen? I'll bring it back tomorrow. The government may bring back capital punishment. Her singing brings back memories of my mother. That brings it all back to me* (= *reminds me of it*).

bring down *vt sep* to cause to fall: *The storm brought all the trees down. (fig) That will bring down the dictator.*

bring forth *vt sep (formal)* to give birth to or produce.

bring forward *vt sep* **1** *(formal: also* **put forward***)* to bring to people's attention; to cause to be discussed *etc*: *They will consider the suggestions which you have brought/ put forward. If you want us to consider your proposal bring it forward at the next meeting.* **2** to cause to happen at an earlier date; to advance in time: *They have brought forward the date of their wedding. They have brought it forward by one week.*

bring in *vt sep* **1** to introduce: *They will bring in a parliamentary bill.* **2** to produce as profit: *His books are bringing in thousands of dollars.* **3** (of a jury) to pronounce or give (a verdict): *They brought in a verdict of guilty.*

bring off *vt sep (inf)* to achieve (something attempted): *I never thought they'd bring it off! They brought off an unexpected victory.*

bring on *vt sep* **1** to cause to come on: *Bring on the dancing girls!* **2** to help to develop: *His illness was brought on by not eating enough.*

bring out *vt sep* **1** to make clear; to reveal: *He brought out the weaknesses of her theory.* **2** to publish: *He brings a new book out every year.*

bring round *vt usually sep* **1** to bring back from unconsciousness: *The smelling-salts brought him round.* **2** to persuade: *We'll bring him round to the idea.*

bring to *vt oblig sep* to bring (someone) back to consciousness: *These smelling-salts will bring him to.*

bring up *vt sep* **1** to rear or educate: *She was brought up to behave herself. Her parents brought her up to be polite.* **2** to introduce (a matter) for discussion: *Bring the matter up at the next meeting.*

bristle with *vt fus* to be full of: *The warship was bristling with guns. The streets were bristling with tourists.*

brush aside *vt sep* to pay no attention to: *She brushed aside my objections. She brushed them aside rudely.*

brush away *vt sep* to wipe off: *She brushed away a tear. She brushed it away.*

brush on *vt sep* to put (paint *etc*) on with a brush.

brush up *vi, vt sep* to refresh one's knowledge of (eg a language): *He brushed up his Spanish before he went on holiday. I must brush up on British history. I'll have to brush up a bit before the exam.*

bubble over *vi* **1** to boil over: *The milk bubbled over.* **2** *(fig)* to be full (with happiness, excitement *etc*): *She was bubbling over with excitement at the news.*

buck up **1** *vi (inf)* to hurry: *You'd better buck up if you want to catch the bus.* **2** *vi, vt sep (inf)* to cheer up: *The good news will buck her up. She bucked up when she heard the news.* **3** *vi, vt sep (inf)* to improve (one's attitude *etc*): *Buck up your ideas or you'll be out of a job.*

buckle down *vi (inf)* to begin (something) seriously: *You must just buckle down to the new job. Just buckle down and get on with it.*

buckle to *vi (inf)* to begin to work seriously: *You must buckle to or go.*

build on **1** *vt sep* to add on by building: *The hospital is bigger now — they built a new wing on in 1977.* **2** *vt fus* to use (a previous success *etc*) as a basis from which to develop: *You've had some success — you must build on it now.* **3** *vt* to base (hopes, success *etc*) on (something): *I've built all my hopes on this book being published.*

build up 1 *vi, vt sep* to increase (the size, extent of): *The traffic begins to build up around five o'clock. They built the wall up gradually.* (fig) *Don't build up the child's hopes — he may not get a present.* **2** *vt sep* to strengthen gradually (a business, one's health, reputation *etc*): *His father built up that grocery business from nothing. Good food and fresh air will help build the child up.* **3** *vt sep* to speak with great enthusiasm about (someone): *They built him up until I couldn't wait to meet him.*

bum around *vi (Amer sl)* to wander or travel around, usually without a (regular) job: *I spent last year bumming around in Europe.*

bump into *vt fus (inf)* to meet (someone) by accident: *I bumped into him the other day in the street.*

bump off *vt sep (sl)* to kill: *The hero got bumped off half-way through the play.*

bunch up *vi, vt sep* to come or put together in bunches, folds or groups: *The sewing-machine went wrong and started to bunch up the material. Traffic often bunches up on a motorway.*

bundle up *vt sep* to make into bundles: *Bundle up all your things and bring them with you.*

buoy up *vt sep* to keep afloat: *The boat has huge tanks full of air which buoy it up.* (fig) *It is cruel to buoy up his hopes if he's going to fail.*

burn down *vi, vt sep* to destroy or be destroyed (completely) by fire: *Our house has burned down. If you smoke in bed you might burn the house down.*

burn out *vi* to become completely extinguished; to be no longer burning: *The flames have burned out now.*

burst into/through *vt fus* to come or go suddenly or violently: *He burst into the room. The house burst into flames. She burst into tears/song. The gunman burst through the door.*

burst out *vt fus* to begin (to do something) suddenly and noisily: *He burst out laughing.*

bustle about *vi* to busy oneself (often noisily or fussily): *She bustled about doing things all day.*

10

butt in *vi (inf)* to interrupt or interfere: *Don't butt in while I'm speaking!*

butt into *vt fus (inf)* to interrupt (a conversation *etc*).

butter up *vt sep (inf)* to flatter (someone) because one wants him to do something for one: *He's always buttering up the boss because he wants promotion. He butters her up because she has a lot of money.*

button up *vi, vt sep* to fasten by means of buttons: *The coat buttons up to the neck. Button your jacket up!*

buy in *vt sep* to buy a stock or supply of: *Have you bought in enough bread for the weekend?*

buy off *vt sep* to bribe: *The gangster's friends bought off the police witness.*

buy out *vt sep* to buy completely (a company's shares *etc*): *The large company expanded by buying out several smaller ones.*

buy up *vt sep* to buy (things) in large quantities: *I've bought up all the houses in this street.*

C

call for *vt fus* **1** to demand or require: *This calls for quick action. Was your rudeness really called for?* **2** to collect: *I'll call for you at eight o'clock.*

call in *vt sep* **1** to ask to come: *Call in the doctor!* **2** to request the return of: *The Board of Commissioners of Currency has called in all the old one-dollar notes.*

call off **1** *vi, vt sep* to cancel: *The party's been called off. She accepted the invitation to the party, but called off at the last minute. They called it off.* **2** *vt sep* to order (a dog *etc*) to stop attacking someone: *He called off the dogs before they really injured their victims.*

call on **1** *vt fus* to visit: *I'll call on our new neighbour tomorrow.* **2** *vt fus (also **call upon**: formal)* to summon or gather together: *call on all one's resources.* **3** *vt fus (also **call upon**)* to appeal to: *They called on God for* *help.* **4** *vt sep* to order to come forward: *I stopped my car at the halt-sign, but the policeman called me on.* **5** *vt fus* (*also* **call upon**: *formal*) to ask (someone) formally (to do something): *The chairman called on each of the four candidates to speak in turn.*

call out *vt sep* **1** to instruct workers to come on strike: *The union has called out the electricity workers.* **2** to summon or bring into operation: *The army was called out to deal with the riot.*

call up *vt sep* **1** to call to service especially in the armed forces. **2** to bring to memory; to recall: *Seeing the children playing called up memories of my own childhood.* **3** to telephone (someone): *He called his mother up from the airport.*

calm down *vi, vt usually sep* to make or become calm: *He tried to calm her down by giving her some brandy. Calm down!*

camp up *vt sep* (*inf*) to make (something) camp: *They camped up the original play so much that it was unrecognizable.*

care for *vt fus* **1** to look after (someone): *The nurse will care for you from now on.* **2** to be fond of: *I don't care for him enough to marry him. I don't care for flowers very much.*

carry forward *vt sep* to add on (a number from one column of figures to the next): *I forgot to carry the 2 forward.*

carry off *vt sep* **1** to take away by carrying: *She carried off the screaming child. She carried it off quickly.* **2** to succeed in (a difficult situation *etc*): *It was a difficult moment, but he carried it off well.*

carry on 1 *vi* to continue: *They must carry on working. Carry on with your work.* **2** *vt sep* to manage (a business *etc*): *He carries on a business as a greengrocer.* **3** *vi* (*inf*) to behave badly: *The children always carry on when the teacher's out of the classroom.* **4** *vi* (*inf derog*) to have a love affair with: *She's been carrying on with the milkman.*

carry out *vt sep* to accomplish or (successfully) finish: *He carried out the plan successfully.*

carry over *vi, vt sep* to continue (into the following page, time *etc*): *We'll have to carry this discussion over into tomorrow. You must carry that word over into the next line. She carried the child over (the river).*

carry through *vt sep (formal)* 1 to help to continue: *Your support will carry me through.* 2 to complete or accomplish: *Now that you have begun the task you must carry it through to the end.*

cart around *vt sep (inf)* to carry around, often with difficulty: *She had to cart her luggage around all day.*

cart off *vt sep (inf)* to carry away, usually impolitely or abruptly: *They carted him off to jail.*

carve out *vt sep (inf)* to achieve or gain (something): *He carved out a career for himself.*

carve up *vt sep (sl)* 1 to divide (money, business *etc*): *We're going to carve up the profits between ourselves.* 2 to cut (a person) with a knife, usually badly: *The criminals really carved the old man up.*

cash in *vt sep* to exchange for money: *I've cashed in all my shares. He had an insurance policy with our company but he has cashed it in.*

cash in on *vt fus (inf)* to make money or other types of profit by taking advantage of (a situation *etc*): *He is the sort of person who cashes in on other people's misfortunes.*

cast off 1 *vi, vt sep* to untie (the mooring lines of a boat). 2 *vt sep (also* **cast aside***) (often fig)* to throw away as unwanted: *He's cast off all his previous business connections. Her husband cast her aside for another woman.* 3 *vi, vt sep* in knitting, to finish (the final row of stitches).

cast on *vi, vt sep* in knitting, to make the first row of stitches.

cast up *vt sep* to raise as an unpleasant reminder: *She's always casting up my failures to me.*

catch on *vi (inf)* 1 to become popular: *Long dresses have really caught on.* 2 to understand: *He's a bit slow to* *catch on. I suddenly caught on to what she was meaning.*

catch out *vt sep* **1** to put out (a batsman) at cricket by catching the ball after it has been hit and before it touches the ground. **2** to cause (someone) to fail or to be unsuccessful by asking him to do something that is too difficult *etc*: *The last question in the exam caught them all out.*

catch up **1** *vi, vt sep* to come level (with) and sometimes overtake: *We caught him up at the corner although he was walking very fast. Ask the taxi-driver if he can catch up with that lorry. We waited for him to catch up.* **2** *vi* to do or finish what has not been done but which ought to have been: *I'll not be able to catch up with my work now. She had a lot of schoolwork to catch up on after her illness. I'll try to catch up with the rest of the class* (= do the work that they have done). **3** *vt sep* to take hastily: *I caught up my cases and dashed to the railway station but I missed the train.*

chalk up *vt sep* **1** to write (something) with chalk on a blackboard *etc*: *The teacher chalked up the answer on the blackboard.* **2** *(fig)* to score (a victory *etc*): *He chalked up three wins in a row.* **3** to note (the cost of something) as being owed by (someone): *Chalk up all these drinks to me.* **4** to think or say (something) has been caused by a particular thing; to ascribe: *You can't chalk his bad work up to lack of trying.*

chance on/upon *vt fus (formal)* **1** to meet by accident: *I chanced on a friend of yours in the library.* **2** to discover by accident: *I chanced upon some information that will interest you.*

change into **1** *vt fus* to remove (clothes *etc*) and replace them by (clean or different ones): *I'll change into an old pair of trousers.* **2** *vt fus, vt* to make into or become (something different): *He's changed into a fine young man. The prince was changed into a frog.*

check in **1** *vi* to arrive (at a hotel) and sign the register: *We checked in last night.* **2** *vt sep* to book a room (for someone at a hotel): *He checked us in at the Mandarin Hotel.*

3 *vt sep* to hand in (*eg* one's baggage at an airport terminal): *We'll check in our luggage, and go and have a meal.*

check out 1 *vi* to leave (a hotel), paying one's bill *etc*: *You must check out before 12 o'clock.* **2** *vt sep* to test or examine: *I'll check out your version of the events.*

check up on *vt fus* to investigate to see if (someone or something) is reliable, honest, true *etc*: *Have you been checking up on me?*

cheer up *vi, vt sep* to make or become more cheerful: *He cheered up when he saw her. The flowers will cheer her up. Do cheer up and try to smile.*

chew over *vt sep (inf)* to think or talk about (a problem *etc*): *He chewed it over for a long time and then decided not to go. He chewed over the problem.*

chicken out *vi (sl)* to avoid doing something due to cowardice: *He chickened out of accepting the challenge. He chickened out at the last minute.*

chime in *vi (inf)* to break into a conversation: *He chimed in with a stupid remark.*

chip in *vi (inf)* **1** to interrupt: *He chipped in with a remark.* **2** to give (money): *He'll chip in with a fiver.*

chop down *vt sep* to cause (especially a tree) to fall by cutting it with an axe: *He chopped down the fir tree.*

chuck up *vt sep (sl)* to abandon (an idea, project *etc*): *He chucked up his university course.*

chum up *vi (inf)* to become friends: *Her son has chummed up with some very badly-behaved children.*

churn out *vt sep (inf often derog)* to produce continuously (usually similar things): *He's been churning out bad plays for ten years now. If he has to churn out so much work each day the quality will be poor.*

clam up *vi (inf)* to become silent suddenly: *She clammed up when she discovered he was a policeman. She was in the midst of a conversation when suddenly she clammed up on me.*

clamp down *vi* to stop some activity; to control strictly: *The government clamped down on public spending.*

clean out *vt sep* **1** to clean thoroughly, throwing out all rubbish *etc*: *We'll clean out the sitting-room tomorrow.* **2** *(sl)* to take all (someone's) money: *He was cleaned out by the huge expenses of moving house.*

clean up 1 *vi, vt sep* to clean (a place) thoroughly: *She cleaned (the room) up after they went home. (fig) We're going to clean up this town* (= make it decent and respectable). **2** *vi (sl)* to make a huge profit: *They cleaned up on their business deals.*

clear off 1 *vt sep* to get rid of; to pay (debts *etc*): *You must clear off your account before we give you any more credit.* **2** *vi (inf)* to go away; to leave: *He cleared off without saying a word.*

clear out 1 *vt sep* to get rid of: *He cleared the rubbish out (of the attic).* **2** *vt sep* to make clear, tidy *etc* by emptying, throwing out rubbish *etc*: *He has cleared out the attic.* **3** *vi (inf)* to go away; to leave: *Clear out and leave me alone!*

clear up 1 *vt sep* to make clear, tidy *etc*: *Clear up this mess! (fig) Have you cleared up the misunderstanding?* **2** *vi* to become better, healthier *etc*: *If the weather clears up, we'll go for a picnic. His infection has cleared up now.*

cleave to *vt fus (formal)* **1** to stick to: *Her wet dress cleaved to her body.* **2** *(fig)* to remain faithful to: *I cleave to the principles of honesty and truth.*

climb down 1 *vi, vt fus* to go down or towards the bottom of (a mountain, ladder *etc*) sometimes using the hands and feet: *It was difficult to climb down (the cliff). He climbed down (the ladder) carefully.* **2** *vi* to accept defeat; to take back what one has said: *He eventually climbed down and accepted our decision.*

clock in/on, out/off *vi* **1** to register or record time of arriving at or leaving work: *We clock in/on at 8.30 and clock out/off at 4.30.* **2** *(loosely)* to begin or finish work: *We clock in at 8 o'clock.*

clock up *vt sep* to register on a mileometer *etc*: *I've clocked up eight thousand miles this year in my car.*

close down 1 *vi, vt sep* (of a business) to close permanently:

High levels of taxation have caused many firms to close down. He closed down his firm when he retired. **2** *vi* (of a TV and radio station *etc*) to stop broadcasting for the day.

close in *vi* **1** to come nearer: *The enemy soldiers are closing in (on us).* **2** (of days) to become shorter, with fewer hours of daylight: *In the autumn the days begin to close in.*

close up *vi, vt sep* **1** to come or bring closer together: *He closed up the space between the lines of print.* **2** to shut completely: *He closed up the house when he went on holiday. The seaside café closes up in the winter.*

close with *vt fus (liter)* to begin fighting with: *He closed with the enemy.*

club together *vi* to join together or put money together (as if in a club) for some purpose: *They clubbed together and bought her a present.*

cluster round *vi, vt fus* to group together in clusters: *They clustered round (the door) to watch the arrival of the queen.*

clutter up *vt sep* to fill or cover in an untidy way: *The drawer was cluttered up with scarves and odd gloves.*

comb out *vt sep* **1** to remove (unwanted matter *etc* from hair) by combing: *She combed the mud out (of his hair).* **2** (fig) to remove (unwanted things, people): *They comb out all except the fittest before setting out on the most difficult part of the expedition.* **3** to comb (hair) into a style after it has been set: *The new hairdresser is good at setting my hair but he doesn't comb it out very well.*

come about *vi* to happen: *How did that come about?*

come across 1 *vi* to be understood or appreciated: *His speech came across well.* **2** *vt fus* to meet or find by chance: *He came across some old friends.*

come along *vi* **1** to come with or accompany the person speaking *etc*: *Come along with me! Do come along — I'm in a hurry.* **2** (inf) to progress: *How are things coming along?*

come between *vt fus* to separate or make unfriendly: *We* *shouldn't let a little thing like this come between us.*

come by *vt fus* to get or obtain: *He came by the books in London. How did you come by that black eye?*

come down *vi* to decrease; to become less: *The price of tea has come down. Tea has come down in price. He has come down in the world* (= He is less important, wealthy *etc* than he was).

come forward *vi* to present oneself or bring oneself to notice: *He came forward and gave us vital information. The police asked witnesses of the accident to come forward.*

come from *vt fus* to have been born in, made in *etc*: *She comes from Italy. Where did this old book come from?*

come in for *vt fus* to receive; to be the target for: *She came in for a lot of criticism.*

come into *vt fus* to inherit: *She'll come into all her father's money when he dies.*

come of *vt fus* to happen to or about: *Whatever came of her plans to go to Africa?*

come off *vi* **1** to happen (successfully): *The gamble didn't come off.* **2** to end by being treated in a good, bad *etc* way: *He was unsuccessful at first but he came off quite well in the end.*

come out *vi* **1** to become known: *The truth finally came out.* **2** to be published: *This newspaper comes out once a week.* **3** *(inf)* to strike: *The men have come out (on strike).* **4** (of a photograph) to be developed: *This photograph has come out very well.* **5** to be shown (in a photograph): *You came out very well in the photos he took.* **6** to decide: *He came out in favour of the death penalty.* **7** to be removed: *This dirty mark won't come out.* **8** *(inf)* to be solved: *My calculations don't come out.* **9** *(old)* to make a first appearance in society: *The elder daughter came out last year.*

come out in *vt fus* to show or develop: *You've come out in spots!*

come out with *vt fus* *(inf)* to say: *What will the child come out with next?*

come round *vi* 1 to visit: *Come round and see us soon.* 2 to regain consciousness: *He won't come round for twenty minutes at least.* 3 to be persuaded, or to persuade oneself, to accept (something): *He'll come round eventually (to your way of thinking).*

come through *vi, vt fus* (of people) to stay alive or survive (something): *Will he come through all right after the operation? He came through the war uninjured.*

come to 1 *vi* to regain consciousness: *When will he come to after the operation?* 2 *vt fus* (only with it as subject) to have the idea or thought (that): *It suddenly came to me that he was the murderer.*

come upon *vt fus* (liter or formal) to meet, find or discover by chance: *I came upon a strange man in the park. She came upon a solution to the problem.*

come up to *vt fus* to reach: *This piece of work doesn't come up to your usual high standard.*

come up with *vt fus* to think of; to produce: *He's come up with a great idea.*

comment on *vt fus* to make a remark *etc* about: *He commented on the disgusting mess in the house.*

conjure up *vt sep* (formal) 1 to bring up in the mind (a picture *etc*): *His description of the holiday conjured up a picture of long, hot days by the sea.* 2 to make appear (as if) from nothing (especially the spirits of dead people, devils *etc*): *He conjured up the spirit of her dead mother.* (fig) *When we arrived unexpectedly she conjured up a meal from some vegetables and a piece of ham.*

contend with *vt fus* to struggle against: *He's contending with problems of all kinds.*

contribute to *vt fus* to help to cause to happen: *His gambling contributed to his downfall.*

cook up *vt sep* (inf) to invent or make up a false story *etc*: *I cooked up a story about my car having broken down. How long did it take you to cook it up?*

cool down *vi, vt sep* 1 to make or become less warm: *Let your food cool down a bit! Put it in the fridge to cool it* *down.* **2** to make or become less excited or less emotional: *He was very angry but he's cooled down a bit now. Her apology cooled him down a bit.*

cool off *vi, vt sep* **1** to make or become less warm: *I'm going to have a cold shower and cool off. A cold shower will cool me off.* **2** to become less enthusiastic, less emotional *etc*: *He used to love her very much but he has cooled off now.*

coop up *vt sep* to shut into a small place: *We've been cooped up in this tiny room for hours. If you coop children up they become naughty.*

cordon off *vt sep* to enclose with a cordon: *The police cordoned off the area where the gunman was last seen. They have cordoned it off.*

cotton on *vi (inf)* to begin to understand: *He'll soon cotton on (to what you mean).*

cough up 1 *vt sep* to produce by coughing; to remove from the throat, chest *etc* by coughing: *He must be very ill — he's coughing up blood. Try and cough up the mucus. I can't cough it up.* **2** *vi, vt sep (sl)* to pay (money): *I can't afford that dress — perhaps mother will cough up (the money) for it.*

count against 1 *vt fus* to be a disadvantage to (someone): *Your previous criminal record will count against you in this trial.* **2** *vt (usually in neg)* to take (a disadvantage) into consideration: *I don't like him but I won't count that against him when I'm considering him for the job.*

count in *vt usually sep* to include: *Have you counted John in? If you're going to the cinema, count me in.*

count on/*(formal)* **upon** *vt fus* to rely on (a person or happening): *I'm counting on you to persuade her. I'm counting on the train's being empty so that I can get a seat.*

count out 1 *vt usually sep* not to include: *If you're going to the cinema, you can count me out.* **2** *vt sep* to say that (a boxer) is the loser because he cannot get up within a count of ten seconds: *He was counted out in the fourth round.*

couple together *vt sep* **1** to join together: *The coaches were coupled together, and the train set off.* **2** to associate (people or things) in one's mind: *I always couple Hemingway and Steinbeck together as being typically American writers.*

cover up 1 *vt sep* to put a cover on (something): *Cover up the soup so that the flies don't get at it. The child covered up her dirty dress with her coat.* **2** *vi, vt sep* to hide or conceal (something illegal or dishonest): *Did you think you'd succeeded in covering up all your mistakes?*

cover up for *vt fus (inf)* to try to prevent the dishonest, illegal *etc* deeds of (someone) from being discovered, by concealing the truth, lying *etc*: *He's been covering up for his friend by telling lies.*

crack down on *vt fus* to take strong action against: *The police are cracking down on vandals in this area.*

crack up *vi (usually fig inf)* to break into pieces; to become unable to continue: *If he works as hard as this all the time he'll eventually crack up. He has cracked up under the strain of over-working. His health is slowly cracking up. The whole building is cracking up.*

credit with *vt* to think of (a person or thing) as having: *I don't credit her with much intelligence. Very ordinary objects were sometimes credited with magical powers.*

creep up *vi* to approach slowly and stealthily (often from behind and unseen): *The cat crept up (on the pigeon). (fig) Old age crept up on her before she had done many of the things she hoped to do.*

crop up *vi (inf)* to happen unexpectedly: *I'm sorry I'm late, but something important cropped up.*

cross out *vt sep* to draw a line through: *He crossed out all her mistakes.*

cry off *vi, vt fus (inf)* to cancel, fail to keep (an engagement or agreement): *After promising to come to the party she cried off at the last minute. They cried off the engagement.*

curl up *vi, v refl* to go, move or roll into a position or shape: *She curled (herself) up in the chair. The hedge-*

hog curled up into a ball. The child curled up on the sofa and went to sleep.

curtain off *vt sep* to separate or enclose with a curtain: *She curtained off the alcove.*

cut across *vt fus* **1** to pass in front of, usually interfering with the progress of: *The lorry cut across (the path of) the little car.* **2** to interfere with or disagree with: *His ideas cut across my own on this subject.* **3** to take a shorter route by way of: *He cut across the grass so as not to be late.*

cut back *vi, vt sep* to reduce considerably: *The government cut back on public spending. Spending was cut back by $10 million.*

cut down **1** *vt sep* to cause to fall by cutting: *He has cut down the apple tree.* **2** *vi* to reduce (an amount taken etc): *I haven't given up smoking but I'm cutting down. You must cut down on sugar to lose weight.*

cut in *vi* **1** to interrupt: *She cut in with a remark.* **2** to move sharply in front of one and so interfere with one's progress: *I had to swerve when a lorry cut in in front of me.*

cut off *vt sep* **1** to interrupt or break a telephone connection: *I was cut off in the middle of the telephone call. They cut me off.* **2** to separate: *They were cut off from the rest of the army (by the enemy). They have cut us off.* **3** to stop or prevent delivery of: *They've cut off our supplies of coal. They have cut them off.* **4** to leave (someone) nothing in a will: *He cut his daughters off without a cent. He cut them off without a cent.* **5** to kill or cause to die sooner than is usual or natural: *He was cut off in his prime.*

cut out **1** *vt sep* to break off or divide by cutting; to make (something) by cutting: *The child cut the pictures out (of the magazine). The teacher cut a little man out (of a piece of cardboard). She cut out a little man.* **2** *vi* to stop working, sometimes because of a safety device: *The engines slowed down and finally cut out. My hair-drier cuts out if it gets over-heated.* **3** *vt sep (inf)* to stop or put an end to: *Cut out all the noise! Cut it out!* **4** *vt sep* to stop (especially eating or drinking): *I've cut out smoking. He's cut out cigarettes — I've cut them out too.*

D

dally with *vt fus (old and liter)* to play with or think about in an idle manner: *He dallied with the idea of asking her to marry him.*

dam up *vt sep* **1** to hold back by means of a dam: *The river has been dammed up.* **2** *(also* **dam back***: fig)* to control or hold back: *She tried bravely to dam back her tears.*

damp down *vt sep* to make (a fire) less strong so that it burns slowly (*eg* overnight): *There was little firelight, as I had damped down the fire for the night. (fig) I had the impression he was trying to damp down their enthusiasm.*

dash off 1 *vt sep (formal)* to write *etc* hurriedly and without much care: *I dashed off a letter or two while I was waiting.* **2** *vi (inf)* to leave or move away in a hurry: *I must dash off to the shops before they shut.*

date from *(also* **date back to***) vt fus* to belong to; to have been made, written *etc* at (a certain time): *Their quarrel dates back to last year. Our house dates from the seventeenth century.*

dawn on/*(formal)* **upon** *vt fus* to become suddenly clear to (a person): *It suddenly dawned on me what he had meant.*

deal with *vt fus* **1** to be concerned with; to discuss: *This book deals with methods of teaching English.* **2** to take action about, especially in order to solve a problem, get rid of a person, complete a piece of business *etc*: *I want to deal with this letter before I do anything else. She deals with all the inquiries.*

declare for, against *vt fus (formal)* to say that one supports or opposes (an opinion, group *etc*): *He always declares for the losing-side.*

depend on/*(formal)* **upon** *vt fus* **1** to rely on: *You can't depend on his arriving on time. You can't depend on the weather being fine.* **2** (not usually used with **is, was** *etc* and **-ing**) to rely on receiving necessary (financial) support from: *The school depends for its survival on money from the Church. He depends on his parents for his university fees.* **3** (not usually used with **is, was** *etc* and **-ing**) (of a future happening *etc*) to be decided by: *Whether I come on Tuesday or not depends on the amount of work I get through before then. Our success depends on everyone working hard.*

deprive of *vt* to take something away from: *This move deprived the prisoner of his means of escape. They deprived him of food and drink.*

derive from 1 *vt fus* to come or arise from: *The word derives from an old French word.* **2** *vt* to draw or take from (a source or origin): *He derives his authority from an Act of Parliament. We derive a lot of comfort from his presence.*

descend on/*(formal)* **upon** *vt fus* to make a sudden attack on: *The soldiers descended on the helpless inhabitants of the village. (fig derog) Visitors descend on us* (= come to stay with us) *every summer. (fig) The children descended on the food as soon as they arrived.*

desist from *vt fus (formal)* to stop: *You must desist from this irresponsible behaviour at once!*

detract from *vt fus (formal)* to take away from or lessen, (especially reputation or value): *The crack detracted from the value of the plate. His recent behaviour detracted from my high opinion of him.*

die away *vi* to fade from sight or hearing: *The sound died away into the distance.*

die down *vi* to lose strength or power: *I think the wind has died down a bit.*

die off *vi* to die quickly or in large numbers: *Herds of* *cattle were dying off because of the drought.*

die out *vi* to cease to exist anywhere: *The custom died out during the last century.*

dig in 1 *vi (inf)* to make an energetic start on something, especially eating a meal: *She put a pot of stew on the table and we all dug in.* **2** *vt sep* to put into the soil by digging: *I dug in a whole sackful of peat.*

dig out *vt sep* **1** to get (something or someone) out (of somewhere) by digging: *We had to dig the car out (of the snow). When we got stuck in the snowdrift we had to dig ourselves out.* **2** *(inf)* to find by searching: *I have that newspaper somewhere — I'll have to dig it out.*

dig up *vt sep* **1** to remove by digging: *We dug up that old tree. They dug up a skeleton.* **2** *(inf)* to find or reveal: *I dug up some old magazines you might like.*

dine on *vt fus (formal)* to have for one's dinner: *They dined on lobster and champagne.*

dine out *vi (formal)* to have dinner somewhere other than one's own house *eg* in a restaurant or at the house of friends *etc*: *We are dining out this evening.*

dip into *vt fus* **1** to take something (especially money) from: *I've been dipping into my savings quite a lot recently.* **2** to look briefly at (a book) or to study (a subject) in a casual manner: *I've dipped into his book on Shakespeare, but I haven't read it right through. I dipped into Chinese history while I worked in a library.*

disagree with *vt fus* (of food) to be unsuitable (to someone) and cause pain: *Onions disagree with me.*

discourage from *vt* to persuade against: *The rain discouraged him from going camping.*

discourse on/upon *vt fus (formal)* to talk about.

discriminate between *vt fus* to make or see a difference between (two people or things): *It is sometimes difficult to discriminate between real and pretended cases of need.*

dish out *vt sep (inf)* to distribute or give to people: *He dished out the tarts. (fig) They dished out jobs all round.*

dish up *vi, vt sep (inf)* to place (food) on plates, dishes *etc* ready to be brought to the table: *I'll dish up while you have another drink.*

dispense with *vt fus (formal)* to get rid of or do without: *We could economize by dispensing with two assistants. As our deep-freeze was uneconomical, we dispensed with it.*

dispose of *vt fus (formal or facet)* to get rid of: *He disposed of the arguments against his plan in two sentences. I've disposed of your old coat by giving it to a jumble sale.*

distinguish between *vt fus* to recognize a difference between: *I can't distinguish between the two types — they both look the same to me.*

do away with *vt fus* **1** to get rid of, especially to abolish officially: *They did away with uniforms at that school years ago.* **2** to kill, especially secretly: *He's afraid someone might try to do away with him.*

do down *vt sep* to cheat or overcome in some way: *He enjoys doing other people down.*

do for *vt fus* **1** *(inf)* to kill or cause the end of: *The coming of television did for the cheap cinemas.* **2** to do housework for: *Mrs Brown comes in twice a week to do for us.*

do in *vt sep (inf)* to kill: *The general opinion about the missing woman was that someone had done her in.*

do out *vt sep (inf)* to clean thoroughly: *I spent the morning doing out the living room. The room's tidy — I did it out yesterday.*

do out of *vt (inf)* to prevent from getting, especially by using dishonest methods: *He feels that he has been done out of a rise in salary. It's all a plot to do me out of a day's holiday.*

do without **1** *vt fus, vi* to manage without and accept the lack of (something one wants): *We'll just have to do without a phone. A lot of people have to do without in other ways in order to buy a house. If you don't want to come and get one, you can just do without.* **2** *vt fus* to manage better without having: *I can do without your opinion, if you don't mind. We could have done with-*

out this little problem!

dote on/*(formal)* **upon** *vt fus* to be fond of to an extent which is foolish: *He just dotes on that child!*

double back *vi* to turn and go back the way one came: *The fox doubled back and went down a hole near to where it had started.*

double up 1 *vi, vt sep* to (cause to) fold over suddenly at the waist: *Everyone doubled up with laughter. He received a blow in the stomach which doubled him up.* **2** *vi* to share a bedroom (with someone else): *The house was so full some of the guests had to double up.*

doze off *vi* to go into a light sleep: *I dozed off in front of the television.*

drain away/**off 1** *vt sep* to allow (water *etc*) to run away completely: *We drain off the hot-water system when we leave our holiday cottage for the winter.* **2** *vi* (of water *etc*) to run away completely: *The flood on the road eventually drained off into the ditch. We let the water drain away.*

draw in *vi* (of a car *etc*) to come to a halt at the side of the road: *Just draw in beyond that yellow car while I post a letter.*

draw off *vt sep* to pour out (liquid) from a large container: *He drew off a pint of water from the tank to examine its purity. The barman drew off a pint of beer.*

draw on 1 *vt fus* (*also* **draw upon**) to use (money, strength, memory *etc*) as a source: *He drew on his imagination for a lot of the details. She's been drawing on her capital for years. He draws on her strength a lot.* **2** *vt sep* to pull on: *He drew on his gloves.* **3** *vi* (*often liter*) to come nearer: *Night drew on and it was soon quite dark.*

draw out 1 *vt sep* to take (money) from a bank: *I drew out a hundred dollars yesterday.* **2** *vt sep* to make long or longer than necessary: *We drew out the journey as much as we could but we still arrived early.* **3** *vi* (of a car *etc*) to move away from the kerb: *A car drew out in front of us as we were overtaking.* **4** *vt sep* to encourage to become less shy, especially to speak: *He sits silently* *in a corner unless someone takes the trouble to draw him out.*

draw up 1 *vi* (of a car *etc*) to stop: *We drew up outside their house.* **2** *vt sep* to arrange in an acceptable form or order: *They drew up the soldiers in line. The solicitor drew up a contract for them to sign.* **3** *vt sep* to move closer: *Draw up a chair!*

dream up *vt sep (derog)* to invent (often taking too much trouble to do so): *He's dreamed up some sort of special recipe for fish. I'm sure she'll dream up some silly plan.*

dress up 1 *vi, vt sep* to put on fancy-dress: *He dressed up as a pirate for the party.* **2** *vi, vt sep* to dress in formal, not casual, clothes: *Don't dress up specially for the party — just come as you are.* **3** *vt sep (inf)* to make (something) appear better, more pleasant *etc* than it is by adding to it *etc*: *We dressed it up when we told him, of course, but the plain fact is that he's useless. You can dress that blouse up with a necklace.*

drink in *vt sep (usually fig)* to take in rapidly or eagerly: *The audience were fascinated, drinking in every expression of his voice.*

drink to *vt fus* to offer good wishes to, or wish well to, while drinking: *Let's drink to that! He gave us some money to drink to his health. Raise your glasses and drink to (the health of) the bride and groom.*

drink up *vi, vt sep* to finish by drinking: *Drink up your milk! We had guests last night and they've drunk up all the beer. Drink up! We must be on our way.*

drive off 1 *vi* to leave or go away in a car *etc*: *He got into a van and drove off.* **2** *vt sep* to keep away: *The place where we picnicked was swarming with wasps and we spent most of the time driving them off.* **3** *vi* in golf, to make the first stroke of a hole from the tee.

drive on 1 *vi* to carry on driving (a car *etc*): *Drive on — we haven't time to stop!* **2** *vt oblig sep* to urge strongly forward: *He drove his horse on towards the fence. It was ambition which drove him on.*

drop back *vi* to slow down while walking *etc* so that one ceases to be in the group in which one originally was: *I was tired of being at the front of the crowd so I dropped back to speak to Bill.*

drop by *vi* to visit someone casually and without being invited: *I'll drop by on my way home if I've time.*

drop in 1 *vi* to arrive informally to visit someone: *Do drop in if you happen to be passing!* **2** *vt oblig sep* to leave (something) for someone: *Just drop the book in at my house sometime, when you've finished it!*

drop off 1 *vi, vt fus* to become separated or fall off: *I was trying to open the door when the door-handle dropped off. I think this button has just dropped off your coat.* **2** *vi (inf)* to fall asleep: *I was so tired I dropped off in front of the television.* **3** *vi (inf)* to become less: *Sales have dropped off during the last three months.* **4** *vt usually sep* to take (someone *etc*) somewhere in a vehicle, leave him *etc* and go on to somewhere else: *I'll drop you off at your house — I'll be going past it on my way home.*

drop out *vi* to withdraw, especially from a course at university *etc* or from the normal life of society: *There are only two of us going to the theatre now Mary has dropped out. She's dropped out of college.*

drum in *vt sep* to force someone to remember (something) by repeating it constantly: *You never remember anything unless I drum it in.*

dry off *vi, vt sep* to make or become completely dry (especially something which is not very wet or only wet on the surface): *She climbed out of the bath and dried herself off.*

dry out 1 *vi, vt sep* to make or become completely dry (especially something which is soaked through): *It'll take ages to dry out your gloves! They can dry out in front of the fire.* **2** *vt sep (fig inf)* to cure or make better (an alcoholic): *He went to a nursing-home to be dried out.*

dry up 1 *vi* (of a liquid or of a source of liquid) to cease completely to be or provide liquid: *The river dried up in the heat. (fig) All my normal sources of news have* *dried up. Supplies of food for the refugees have dried up sooner than expected.* **2** *vt sep* to make dry: *The sun dried up the puddles in the road.* **3** *vi (inf)* to forget what to say, *eg* in a play: *He dried up in the middle of the scene.*

dust down *vt sep* **1** to brush in order to remove the dust from: *She picked herself up and dusted herself down.* **2** *(fig inf)* to reprimand or scold: *He dusted his staff down about the drop in their efficiency.*

dwell on/*(formal)* **upon** *vt fus* to think or speak about (something) for a long time: *It doesn't help to dwell on your problems for too long. He dwelt at length in his speech on various approaches to the subject.*

E

ease off *vi* to make or become less strong, less severe, less tight, less fast *etc*: *The pain has eased off. The driver eased off as he approached the town.*

eat into *vt fus* to destroy or waste gradually: *Acid eats into metal. The school fees have eaten into our savings.*

egg on *vt sep (inf)* to urge (somebody) on (to do something): *He egged on his friend to steal the radio. She egged him on to apply for a better job.*

eke out *vt sep* **1** to make (a supply of something) last longer *eg* by adding something else to it: *You could eke out the meat with potatoes.* **2** to manage with difficulty to make (a living, livelihood *etc*): *The artist could scarcely eke out a living from his painting.*

elaborate on/*(formal)* **upon** *vt fus* to discuss details of: *She elaborated on the next day's menu. The headmaster elaborated upon the idea for a new school uniform.*

embark on/*(formal)* **upon** *vt fus* to start or engage in: *They embarked on a war against the French. She embarked on a new career.*

encroach on/upon *vt fus (formal)* **1** to advance into (someone else's land *etc*): *In making his garden larger, he encroached on Mr Brown's wood.* **2** to remove part of (someone's right, privilege *etc*) unjustly: *Is the Government slowly encroaching on the liberty of the individual?*

end up *vi* **1** to reach or come to an end, usually unpleasant: *I knew he would end up in jail. He ended up in hospital. We ended up without enough money to pay our bus fare home.* **2** to end; to finish; to do something in the end: *He said he would not go but he ended up by going. He refused to believe her but he ended up apologizing.*

enlarge on/upon *vt fus (formal)* to speak, write *etc* in more detail: *Would you like to enlarge on your original statement? He enlarged upon his holiday plans.*

enter into *vt fus* **1** to take part in: *He entered into an agreement with the film director.* **2** to take part enthusiastically in: *They entered into the Christmas party spirit.* **3** to begin to discuss: *We cannot enter into the question of salaries yet.* **4** to be part of: *The price did not enter into the discussion.*

enter on/upon *vt fus (formal)* to begin: *We have entered upon the new term.*

enthuse over/about *vt fus (inf)* to be enthusiastic about: *I couldn't enthuse over the new baby. He is constantly enthusing about his new job.*

even out **1** *vi* to become level or regular: *The road rose steeply and then evened out. His irregular heartbeats began to even out.* **2** *vt sep* to make smooth or equal: *He raked the soil to even it out.* **3** *vt sep* to make equal: *If Jane would do some of Mary's typing, that would even the work out.*

even up *vt sep* to make equal: *John did better in the maths exam than Jim and that evened up their marks.*

explain away *vt sep* to get rid of (difficulties *etc*) by clever explaining: *She tried to explain away the fact that the money was missing by saying it had been stolen. How did she explain it away?*

exult in/at *vt fus* *(formal)* to be very happy about; to rejoice at: *They exulted in their victory. They exulted at the news of their victory.*

exult over *vt fus* *(formal)* to triumph over; to be happy because one has defeated (someone): *She exulted over her rival.*

F

face up to *vt fus* to meet or accept boldly: *He faced up to his difficult situation.*

fade out *vi, vt sep* (of sound, a film picture *etc*) to (cause to) grow faint and disappear: *The last scene of the film faded out and the lights came on. The radio engineer faded out the sound too early.*

fall apart *vi* to break into pieces: *My bicycle is falling apart.*

fall away *vi* 1 to become less in number: *The crowd began to fall away.* 2 to slope downwards: *The ground fell away steeply.*

fall back *vi* to move back or stop coming forward: *The men following him fell back as he turned to face them.*

fall back on *vt fus* *(inf)* to use, or to go for help, finally when everything else has been tried: *Whatever happens you have your father's money to fall back on.*

fall behind 1 *vi, vt fus* to be slower than (someone else): *Hurry up! You're falling behind (the others). (fig) He is falling behind in his schoolwork.* 2 *vi* to become late in regular payment, letter-writing *etc*: *Don't fall behind with the rent!*

fall down *vi* (sometimes with **on**) to fail (in): *That's the point where his plans fall down — he hasn't said what we're to do if he's out. He's falling down on his job.*

fall for *vt fus* *(inf)* 1 to be deceived by (something): *I made up a story to explain why I had not been at work and he* *fell for it.* **2** to fall in love with (someone): *He has fallen for your sister.*

fall in with *vt fus* **1** to join with (someone) for company: *On the way home we fell in with some friends.* **2** to agree with (a plan, idea *etc*): *They fell in with our suggestion.*

fall off *vi* to become smaller in number or amount: *Theatre audiences often fall off during the summer.*

fall on/(*formal*) **upon** *vt fus* to attack: *He fell on the old man and beat him. They fell hungrily upon the food.*

fall out *vi* (*inf*) to quarrel: *I have fallen out with my brother. She and her friends are always falling out.*

fall through *vi* (of plans *etc*) to fail or come to nothing: *We had planned to go to Paris, but the plans fell through.*

fall to 1 *vi* (*old*) to begin enthusiastically, especially eating: *The food was put on the table and they fell to eagerly.* **2** *vt fus* (*formal: only with* it *as subject*) to come as one's duty *etc*: *It falls to me to take care of the children.*

fan out *vi, vt sep* to spread out in the shape of a fan: *He fanned out the photographs in his hand. The crowd fanned out across the square.*

fasten on/(*formal*) **upon** *vt fus* to seize on or fix one's attention on: *He fastened (up)on her last remark.*

fatten up *vi, vt sep* to make or become fat: *They are fattening up a chicken to eat at Christmas. That pig is fattening up well.*

fawn upon *vt fus* (*liter: derog*) to be too humble or to flatter (someone) in a servile way: *The courtiers fawned upon the king.*

feel for *vt fus* (*formal*) **1** to be sympathetic with: *She felt for him in his sorrow.* **2** to try to find by feeling: *She felt for a pencil in her handbag.*

ferret about *vi* (*inf*) to search busily and persistently: *He ferreted about in the cupboard. What are you ferreting about in that drawer for?*

ferret out *vt sep* (*inf*) to find out after a search: *He managed to ferret out a very interesting piece of news.*

He ferreted it out after a very long search.

fiddle with *vt fus* to make restless, aimless movements: *Stop fiddling with your pencil!*

fight back *vi* to use (physical) violence against someone who is using (physical) violence against one: *If he hits you, fight back.*

fight off *vt sep* to drive (someone or something) away by using (physical) violence: *They fought off the enemy with machine-guns. (fig) I'll fight this cold off by going to bed early.*

fight out *vt oblig sep* to fight on to a decisive end: *Although they were both exhausted the armies fought it out until the attackers were victorious at dawn. (fig) Fight it out among yourselves which of you is to go.*

figure out *vt sep (inf)* to understand: *I can't figure out why he said that. I just can't figure it out.*

fill in 1 *vt sep* to add or put in (whatever is needed to make something complete): *The teacher drew outlines of animals and the children filled them in. I've got a general idea of what happened — could you fill in the details?* **2** *vt sep* to complete (forms, applications *etc*) by putting in the information required: *Have you filled in your tax form yet? You must fill in this form if you want a new passport. Have you filled it in correctly?* **3** *vt oblig sep* to give (someone) all the necessary information: *I've been away — can you fill me in on what has happened?* **4** *vt sep* to occupy (time): *He had several drinks in the bar to fill in time until the train left. Now that I'm not working I have a lot of spare time — I don't know how to fill it in!* **5** *vi (inf)* to do another person's job temporarily: *I'm filling in for his secretary while she's in hospital. He doesn't usually work here — he's just filling in.*

fill out 1 *vi, vt sep* to (cause to) become rounder or fatter: *She used to be very thin but she has filled out a bit now. Her face has filled out since I last saw her. Eating all that food will certainly fill her out.* **2** *vt sep* to fill in (forms *etc*): *I'm tired of filling out forms.*

fill up *vi, vt sep* to make or become completely full: *Fill up the petrol tank please. Fill it up. The hall filled up quickly.*

film over *vi (formal)* to become covered with a film: *Her eyes gradually filmed over with tears.*

find out 1 *vt sep* to discover: *I found out what was troubling her. When did you find it out?* 2 *vt oblig sep* to discover the truth (about someone), usually that he has done wrong: *He had been stealing for years, but eventually they found him out.*

finish off *vt sep* 1 to complete: *He finished off the job yesterday.* 2 to use, eat *etc* the last of: *We've finished off the pudding.* 3 *(inf usually facet)* to kill (a person): *His last illness nearly finished him off.*

finish up 1 *vt sep* to use, eat *etc* the last of; to finish: *Finish up your meal as quickly as possible. I have finished it up. We've finished up all the red paint.* 2 *vi* to end: *It was no surprise to me when he finished up in jail. The car finished up in the dump.*

finish with *vt fus* to stop being fond of: *They used to be friendly but they've finished with each other now. He used to collect stamps but he's finished with that hobby now.*

fire away *vi* 1 to begin to fire guns *etc*: *'Fire away!' called the sergeant-major to the young soldiers.* 2 *(inf)* to go ahead: *I'm ready to start writing down what you're going to say — fire away!* 3 to continue shooting for some time: *They fired away at the target for several minutes.*

fish out *vt sep (inf)* to pull (something) out with some difficulty: *At last he fished out the letter he was looking for.*

fit in *vi* to be able to live, exist *etc* in agreement or harmony: *The girl is unhappy at school — she just doesn't fit in (with the rest of the children). My holiday plans must fit in with my colleague's plans.*

fit out *vt sep* to provide with everything necessary (clothes, equipment *etc*): *The climbers were fitted out for their* expedition by the best shop in town. *The shop fitted them out at very short notice. The ship left dock after it was fitted out.*

fix on/(*formal*) **upon** *vt fus* to decide or to choose: *Have you fixed on a date for your party yet?*

fix up *vt sep* to arrange; to settle: *We fixed up a meeting for next week.*

fizzle out *vi (inf)* to fail; to come to nothing: *The fire eventually fizzled out. Their plans to go abroad fizzled out when they realized how expensive the trip would be.*

flag down *vt sep* to wave at (a car *etc*) in order to make it stop: *We flagged down a taxi in the High Street. You might be able to flag a taxi down.*

flake off *vi, vt fus* to come off in flakes: *The girl's skin is flaking off. The paint is flaking off (that door).*

flare up *vi* suddenly to burn brightly: *A sudden wind made the fire flare up. (fig) A quarrel flared up between them. (fig) The spots on his face flared up again.*

flash by/past *vi* to pass quickly: *The days flashed by. The cars flashed past.*

flatten down *vt sep* to make (something) flat: *The wind had flattened down the farmer's wheat.*

flatten out *vi, vt sep* to make or become flat: *He flattened out the bent metal. The countryside flattened out as they came near the sea.*

flirt with *vt fus* to behave towards (someone) as though one were in love, but without serious intentions: *She flirts with every man she meets. (fig) She flirts with the idea of going to America.*

flock to/into *vt fus* to gather or go somewhere together in a crowd: *We all flocked into the dining-room. People flocked to the football match.*

flog away *vi (sl)* to work very hard: *He flogged away at his homework.*

flounce out/away *vi* to move (out, away) in anger, impatience *etc*: *She flounced out (of the room). She flounced away in a temper.*

fluff out/up *vt sep* to make full and soft like fluff: *The bird fluffed out its feathers. Fluff up the pillows and make the invalid more comfortable.*

flush out *vt sep* to cause (an animal *etc*) to leave a hiding place: *The hounds flushed out the fox from the woods. The police soon flushed out the criminal.*

fog up *vi, vt sep* to cover with fog *etc*: *Her glasses were fogged up with steam.*

follow up *vt sep* **1** to go further in doing something: *I like painting, so I decided to follow it up. He has never followed up his original interest in the subject. The police are following up a clue.* **2** to find out more about (something): *I heard the news about him, and decided to follow it up.*

fool about/around *vi* to act like a fool or playfully: *Every time I see him he seems to be fooling around. Stop fooling about with that knife!*

forage about *vi (inf)* to search thoroughly: *He foraged about in the cupboard.*

forbear from *vt fus (formal)* to keep oneself from (doing something): *We must forbear from talking about it.*

fork out *vi, vt sep (inf)* to pay usually unwillingly; to hand over (usually money): *I'll have to fork out the cost of the meal. I've forked out enough money on this holiday already but I suppose I'll have to fork more out. Do I have to fork out again?*

freeze up *vi, vt sep* to stop moving or functioning because of extreme cold: *The car engine froze up and wouldn't start.* (*fig*) *The actor was so nervous that he froze up* (= could not speak his lines). *The cold weather has frozen up the gate — it won't open!*

freshen up *vi, vt sep* to (cause to) become less tired or untidy looking: *I must freshen up before dinner. A wash and a rest will freshen me up.*

fritter away *vt sep* to throw away or waste gradually: *He frittered away all his money on gambling. She frittered away her time in going to the cinema instead of studying.*

frost over/up *vi* to become covered with frost: *The fields* *frosted over during the night. The windscreen of my car frosted up last night.*

frown on/upon *vt fus (formal)* to disapprove of (something): *My family frowns (up)on smoking and drinking.*

G

gad about/around *vi (inf derog)* to go around to one place after another (usually in order to amuse oneself): *She's forever gadding about now that the children are at school.*

gain by/from *vt* to get (something good, *eg* money) by doing something: *What have I to gain by staying here?*

gain on/(formal) upon *vt fus* to get or come closer to (a person, thing *etc* that one is chasing): *Drive faster — the police car is gaining on us.*

gallop through *vt fus (inf)* to do, say *etc* (something) very quickly: *He galloped through his homework so that he could watch television.*

gamble away *vt sep* to lose (a sum of money) by gambling unsuccessfully: *He got $5000 from his father, but gambled it all away.*

gang up on *vt fus (inf)* to join or act with a person *etc* against (some other person *etc*): *The manager felt that the younger members of staff were ganging up on him.*

gang up with *vt fus (inf)* to join or act with (a person *etc*) for some purpose, *eg* amusement: *The girls ganged up with the boys they met on the beach.*

gasp out *vt sep* to say (something) while out of breath: *The boy ran up and gasped out his story to the policeman.*

gather round *vi* to come together around a person, thing *etc*: *Will everyone please gather round?*

gather together *vi, vt sep* to come or bring together, in a group: *The lecturer gathered his books and papers* *together. He gathered them together. (fig) I had no time to gather my thoughts together before I was asked to speak.*

gather up *vt sep* to collect together by picking up: *He gathered up his books and walked out. He gathered them up.*

gear to *vt* to adapt or design (something) to suit a particular need: *This book has been geared to adult students.*

gen up *vi, vt sep (sl)* to study (something) or get the information one needs (on some subject): *I'll have to gen up on the rules of debating if I'm to be the chairman. Will you gen me up (on the situation)?*

get about *vi* 1 (of stories, rumours *etc*) to become well known: *I don't know how the story got about that she was leaving.* 2 to be able to move or travel about, often of people who have been ill: *She didn't get about much after her operation. Now that they have sold their car, they don't get about a lot.*

get across *vi, vt usually sep (inf)* to be or make (something) understood: *This is something which rarely gets across to the general public. The plan seems quite clear to me, but I just can't get it across (to anyone else).*

get after *vt fus* to follow or chase (a person, thing *etc*): *If you want to catch him, you had better get after him at once.*

get ahead *vi* 1 to make progress; to be successful: *If you want to get ahead, you must work hard.* 2 (with **of**) to make more progress than (someone or something else): *This company intends to get ahead of all its rivals.*

get along *vi (inf)* 1 to manage or make progress: *I can't get along without some help. How are things getting along?* 2 (often *with* **with**) to be friendly or on good terms (with someone): *I get along very well with him. The children just cannot get along together.* 3 to move or go away (often to some other place): *I must be getting along now or I'll miss the bus.*

get around 1 *vi* (of stories, rumours *etc*) to become well known: *I don't know how the story got around that she* *was leaving.* **2** *vi (inf)* (of people) to be active or involved in many activities: *He really gets around, doesn't he!* **3** *vt fus* to avoid or solve (a problem *etc*): *I don't see any way of getting around these difficulties.*

get at *vt fus* **1** to reach (a place, thing *etc*): *The farm is very difficult to get at. The hole is too deep for me to get at the ring I dropped. (fig) Somehow or other, I'll get at the truth. Whatever you say, I must get at the books in your room.* **2** *(inf)* to suggest or imply (something): *What are you getting at?* **3** *(inf)* to point out (a person's faults) or make fun of (a person): *He's always getting at me.* **4** *(inf)* to persuade (a person) by money, threats *etc* to tell lies *etc*: *The witnesses have been got at.*

get away **1** *vi (often with* **from***)* to (be able to) leave: *I usually get away (from the office) at five.* **2** *vi* to escape: *The thieves got away in a stolen car.* **3** *vi, vt oblig sep (inf)* (of a letter *etc*) to post or be posted: *I must get this letter away tonight. This letter must get away tonight.* **4** *vt oblig sep (inf: with* **from***)* to take (something) away (from a person *etc*): *I must get that letter away from her before she reads what I said about her.* **5** *vi (with* **from***: usually in neg)* to deny (something) or avoid taking (something) into consideration: *There is no getting away from the fact that John is not the right man for the job. He's a clever man — there's no getting away from it/that.*

get away with *vt fus* to do (something bad) without being punished for it: *Murder is a serious crime and one rarely gets away with it.*

get back *vi, vt oblig sep* to move away: *The policeman told the crowd to get back. He managed to get the sheep back from the edge of the cliff.*

get back at *vt fus (inf)* to have revenge on (a person *etc*): *You can laugh now, but I'll get back at you somehow.*

get by *vi (inf)* **1** to manage: *I can't get by on $50 a week.* **2** *(inf)* to be acceptable: *This definition isn't very good but it will probably get by.*

get down **1** *vi (sometimes with* **from***)* to leave (a bus, train *etc*): *The platform is so low that it is difficult to get down (from the train).* **2** *vt oblig sep (inf)* to make (a person) sad: *Working in this place really gets me down.* **3** *vt usually sep* to swallow (usually with difficulty or unwillingly): *I feel sick, but I'll try to get some food down.* **4** *vt sep* to write (something) down: *Did you get down everything he said?*

get down to *vt fus* to begin to work (hard) at (something): *I must get down to work tonight, as I've got exams next week.*

get in *vt sep* **1** to send for (a person): *The television is broken — we'll need to get a man in to repair it.* **2** to manage to give, have *etc*: *I'm hoping to get in a couple of hours' study before dinner. The boxer only managed to get a couple of punches in before the referee stopped the fight.*

get into *vt fus* **1** to put on (clothes *etc*): *I find it very difficult to get into these tight trousers. How on earth did she get into that dress — it's much too tight! Get into your pyjamas.* **2** to (begin to) be in a particular state or behave in a particular way: *He gets into a temper if you argue with him. You'll get into trouble if you break that vase. I don't know what has got into him* (= I don't know why he is behaving the way he is). **3** *(inf)* to begin to enjoy, understand *etc* (a book): *I just can't get into that book.*

get in with *vt fus (inf)* to become friendly or on good terms with (a person), usually for one's own benefit or advantage: *He's trying to get in with the boss in order to get a pay rise.*

get off 1 *vi, vt fus* to leave (a bus, train *etc*): *I get off at the next stop. We all got off the bus.* **2** *vi (inf)* to leave (a place): *I must be getting off now. It's time you got off to school.* **3** *vt oblig sep* to take off or remove (clothes, marks *etc*): *I can't get my boots off. I'll never get these stains off (my dress).* **4** *vi, vt oblig sep (inf: usually with* **with**) to (cause or help someone to) receive little or no punishment (after doing wrong): *The thief got off with* a small fine. *The thief's lawyer got him off with a small fine.* **5** *vt fus (inf)* to manage not to do (something that one doesn't want to do): *I got off digging the garden this week by pretending to feel ill.* **6** *vt fus* to stop talking, writing *etc* about (something); to change (the subject which one is talking, writing *etc* about): *Can we get off this subject, please? We've rather got off the subject.*

get off with *vt fus (sl)* to form a close, often sexual, relationship with (someone), *eg* at a dance, party: *I'm hoping to get off with Mary tonight.*

get on 1 *vi (often with* **in**) to make progress or be successful: *How are you getting on in your new job? It takes intelligence and hard work to get on in life.* **2** *vi (inf) (sometimes with* **with**) to work, live *etc* in a friendly way: *We get on very well together. I get on well with him.* **3** *vi (inf)* to grow old: *Our doctor is getting on a bit now.* **4** *vt oblig sep* to put (clothes *etc*) on: *Go and get your coat on — we're just about to leave.* **5** *vi (inf)* to leave (somewhere) to go somewhere else: *Well, I must be getting on now.* **6** *vi (often with* **with**) to continue doing (something): *I must get on, so please don't interrupt me. I must get on with my work.*

get on at *vt fus (inf)* to criticize (a person) continually or frequently: *My wife is always getting on at me to clean my shoes/for not cleaning my shoes.*

get on to *vt fus* **1** to make contact with (a person *etc*) *eg* by telephone (often because one is displeased with something or to get information about something): *This is the third time this week that my television has broken down — I'll need to get on to the manager about it. You must get on to the airline at once to see if your flight has been delayed.* **2** to deal with (a problem *etc*): *I'll get on to the matter of your television at once.*

get out 1 *vi* to leave or escape: *I'm not interested in your nonsense, so just get out! No-one knows how the lion got out.* **2** *vi (of information)* to become known: *I've no idea how word got out that you were leaving.* **3** *vt sep* to manage to say (something) usually with some difficulty: *I wanted to say I loved her, but I couldn't get the words out.* **4** *vt sep* to prepare and publish (a report, book *etc*): *We'll have to get this pamphlet out before next week.* **5** *vt sep* to borrow (books *etc*) from a library *etc*: *Will you get two books out for me when you go to the library?*

get out of 1 *vt fus* to leave (a car *etc*); to escape (from somewhere): *He got out of the car. The lion got out of its cage unnoticed.* **2** *vt fus, vt* to (help a person *etc* to) avoid doing something: *I wonder how I can get out of washing the dishes. I wonder how I can get him out of going to the party? How can I get him out of it?* **3** *vt (inf)* to persuade or force (a person *etc*) to give someone something: *Somehow or other, I'll get the money/facts out of him.* **4** *vt fus, vt (inf)* to (persuade a person *etc* to) stop doing something which is usually done by that person: *I wish I could get out of the habit of kicking the table. I wish I could get that child out of the habit of sucking his thumb.*

get over 1 *vt fus* to recover from (an illness, disappointment *etc*): *I've got over my cold now.* **2** *vt fus (inf)* to no longer feel sad when thinking about (a person, usually of the opposite sex, with whom one was once very friendly): *It took me a long time to get over my first girl-friend.* **3** *vt usually sep* to manage to make (oneself or something) understood: *We must get our message over to the general public.*

get round *vt fus* **1** *(inf)* to persuade (a person *etc*) to do something he, she *etc* would not wish to do: *She can always get round her grandfather by giving him a big smile.* **2** to solve (a problem *etc*): *We can easily get round these few difficulties.*

get (a)round to *vt fus (inf)* to manage to (do something); to find enough time to (do something): *I don't know when I'll get round to (painting) the door.*

get through 1 *vt fus* to finish (work *etc*): *We've got to get through a lot of work today. We got through a lot of* whisky at the party. **2** vi to make contact (with another person etc) by telephone: *I couldn't get through (to my mother) yesterday.* **3** vi, vt fus (inf) to pass (an examination): *I'll never get through (my French exam).* **4** vt oblig sep to help (a person etc) to pass an examination: *He's a good teacher, but even he couldn't get her through (her French exam).* **5** vi to arrive (somewhere), usually with some difficulty: *The food got through to them despite the enemy's attempts to stop it.* **6** vi, vt fus, vt oblig sep (especially of a bill in Parliament) to (cause to) be agreed or accepted: *The new bill will never get through. The abortion bill has got through Parliament. The government succeeded in getting the bill through.* **7** vi (with **to**) to make oneself understood (by someone): *I just can't seem to get through to her any more.* **8** vt oblig sep to make someone understand (something): *We can't get it through to him that smoking is bad for his health.*

get up 1 vi, vt oblig sep to (cause to) get out of bed: *I got up at seven o'clock. Get me up at seven o'clock. You'll never get John up on time.* **2** vi to stand up: *Please don't get up on my account.* **3** vt sep to increase (usually speed): *The vehicle got up speed as it ran down the hill.* **4** vi (of a wind etc) to begin to be strong, fierce or rough: *There's quite a wind getting up outside.* **5** vt sep (inf) to arrange, organize or prepare (something): *We must get up some sort of celebration for him when he leaves.* **6** vt sep (inf) to cause oneself to feel (an emotion etc): *I just can't get up any enthusiasm for this project.*

get up to vt fus **1** to reach: *So far I've got up to page sixty.* **2** (inf) to do (something bad): *He's always getting up to mischief. What will he get up to next?*

ginger up vt sep (inf) to make (a person etc) more active and lively: *The leaders of the political party decided they would need to ginger up some of their local branches.*

give away vt sep **1** to give, send, present etc (something) to someone (eg because one no longer wants it): *I'm going to give all my money away.* **2** to cause or allow (information, one's plans *etc*) to become known usually accidentally: *Don't give me away. He gave away our hiding-place.*

give back *vt sep* to give to someone (something that he or she gave to one earlier): *She gave me back the book that she borrowed last week. Girls who break their engagements usually give back their engagement rings.*

give in 1 *vi (often with* **to**) to stop fighting and admit that one has been defeated: *The only way to win a war is to keep fighting and never think about giving in (to the enemy). (fig) I give in; I can't solve this riddle.* **2** *vt sep* to hand, bring or present (something) to someone (often a person in authority): *Do we have to give in our books at the end of the lesson?*

give off *vt sep* to produce (something): *That fire is giving off a lot of smoke.*

give out 1 *vt sep* to give (something) usually to several people: *The mayor is giving out the school prizes this year.* **2** *vi (inf)* to come to an end or be used up: *My patience/money gave out.* **3** *vt sep* to send out or produce (something): *The fire burned fiercely, giving out a lot of heat.* **4** *vi (inf) (often with* **on**) to break down, stop working *etc*: *My car engine gave out (on me).* **5** *vt sep* to make (something) known: *It was given out that there would be another wage freeze.*

give over 1 *vt usually sep* to give (a person, thing *etc*) to someone: *He gave his prisoners/the jewels over to the police.* **2** *vi, vt fus (sl)* to stop (doing something): *Give over whistling! Do give over!* **3** *vt usually sep* to be devoted to or used for (some purpose): *This evening will be given over to discussion of this paper.*

give up 1 *vi, vt sep* to stop doing (something) or trying to do (something): *I can't understand this problem — I think I'll give up (trying to solve it). I must give up smoking. We'll have to give up the search until tomorrow.* **2** *vt sep* to stop using, eating, seeing *etc* (a person, thing *etc*): *You'll have to give up cigarettes. He gave them up last year. I won't give up all my hobbies for* *you*. **3** *vt sep* to give (a person, thing *etc*) to (a person *etc*) or allow (a person *etc*) to have (a person, thing *etc*): *Children should give up their seats on the bus if other people are standing. The police called on the thief to give himself up. He gave himself up to the police.* **4** *vt sep* to devote (one's life, time *etc*) to doing something: *I have given up so much of my time to this job that I won't stop now.* **5** *vt usually sep* (*often with* as *or* for) to consider (a person, thing *etc*) to be: *You took so long to arrive that we had almost given you up* (*for lost/as dead*). **6** *v refl sep* (*with* to: *formal*) to do or feel (something) without trying to control (oneself) any longer: *She gave herself up to despair/grief.*

glance off *vi, vt fus* to hit (something) and bounce off to one side: *The ball glanced off the edge of his bat.*

gloss over *vt fus* to try to hide, or to try to prevent anyone noticing (a mistake *etc*): *The chairman tends to gloss over any information that would prove him wrong.*

go about 1 *vi* (*also* **go around**) (of rumours *etc*) to be passed from one person to another: *There's a story going about that you are in debt.* **2** *vt fus* to (begin to) work at (a job, problem *etc*): *I don't know the best way to go about the job. When the Director comes in, just go about your work as normal.* **3** *vi* (of a ship) to change direction or turn around.

go about with *vt fus* (*inf*) to be friendly with and often seen in the company of (a person usually of the other sex): *She goes about with Tom.*

go after *vt fus* (*inf*) **1** to try to get or win (something): *He's going after that prize/job.* **2** to follow or chase (a person *etc*): *Go after him and apologize.*

go against *vt fus* **1** to resist, oppose or refuse to act on (a person's suggestions, wishes *etc*): *A child should never go against his parents' wishes.* **2** to be unacceptable to (a person *etc*) because of his beliefs *etc*: *This goes against my conscience, but I'll have to do it.* **3** to be unfavourable to (a person, thing *etc*): *A gambler should stop gambling when luck is going against him.*

go ahead *vi* (*often with* **and** *or* **with**) to start to do (something): *I warned him not to touch it but he went ahead and did it.* 'Can I borrow this book?' 'Yes, go ahead.' *Can I go ahead with this job now?*

go along *vi* **1** (*often with* **to**) to go (to a meeting, party *etc*): *I'll go along (to the meeting) with you.* **2** to be in the process of doing (something): *I never check my work after I've finished it — I prefer to do the checking as I go along.*

go along with *vt fus* (*inf*) to agree with (a person, suggestion *etc*): *I'm afraid I can't go along with you on that.*

go around *vi* (of stories, rumours *etc*) to be passed from one person to another: *There's a rumour going around that you are leaving.*

go around with *vt fus* (*inf*) to be friendly with and often in the company of (a person): *I don't like the group of friends you're going around with.*

go at *vt fus* (*inf*) **1** to attack (a person *etc*): *The little boys went at each other with their fists.* **2** to do (something) or deal with (a job *etc*) with enthusiasm: *He really went at the job of painting the living room.*

go back *vi* **1** to return or take (a person's or one's own) mind back to an earlier time, topic of conversation *etc*: *Let us go back to the time of Queen Victoria. My memory doesn't go back as far as that. Let's go back for a minute to what we are talking about earlier.* **2** to begin to do something one had stopped doing: *He has gone back to smoking cigars again.*

go back on *vt fus* to fail to do (something one has promised to do): *I never go back on my promises.*

go below *vi* to go below the deck (in a ship).

go by *vt fus* **1** (*inf*) to base an opinion or a judgement on (something): *We can't go by what he says.* **2** (*inf*) to be guided by (something): *When I'm not sure what to do, I always go by the instructions you gave me.* **3** to be known as (something): *His name is Charles but he always goes by the name of Plug.*

go down *vi* (*inf*) **1** (of food) to be swallowed: *Yoghurt* *goes down easily.* **2** to become smaller (because of the loss of air *etc*): *My tyres have gone down. The swelling on my arm has gone down a bit.* **3** *(inf) (with* **well**/**badly**) to be approved or disapproved of: *The story went down well (with them). His jokes went down badly (with the audience).* **4** *(nautical)* (of a ship) to sink: *They were lost at sea when the ship went down.* **5** (of the sun or moon) to go below the horizon. **6** *(with* **in**) to be remembered: *Your bravery will go down in history.* **7** to be written down: *This will all go down in my report.* **8** (of a book) to deal with events as far as (a certain date): *This history book only goes down to the First World War.* **9** *(inf)* (of places) to become less pleasant or desirable: *This part of town has gone down in the last twenty years.*

go down with *vt fus (inf)* to catch (a disease): *He has gone down with flu.*

go for *vt fus* **1** to attack (a person, animal *etc*) physically or in words: *The two dogs went for each other as soon as they met. The newspapers went for the Prime Minister over the Government's tax proposals.* **2** to be attracted by (a person, thing *etc*): *I go for redheads in short skirts.*

go forth *vi (archaic or liter)* to be sent out or announced: *The news went forth that the President had died of a heart attack.*

go in *vi* **1** (of the sun or moon) to become covered by cloud. **2** to begin work: *What time does school go in?*

go in for *vt fus* **1** to take part in (an examination, competition *etc*): *I'm not going in for the 1000 metres race.* **2** to do (something) as a hobby, job, habit *etc*; to study (something) at university *etc*: *My son is going in for medicine. My son goes in for collecting postcards. We don't go in for using people's surnames in this office.*

go into *vt fus* **1** to make a careful study of (something): *We'll need to go into this plan in more detail before we make any decision.* **2** to discuss or describe (something) in detail: *I don't want to go into the problems at the moment as there isn't any time before my next appoint-*

ment. **3** to begin to do (something) as a job: *My son hopes to go into politics.*

go off 1 *vi* (of a gun) to fire; (of a bomb *etc*) to explode: *The little boy was injured when the rifle/firework went off in his hand.* **2** *vi* (*often with* **with**: *often in a bad sense*) to leave: *He went off yesterday. He has gone off with* (= *He has stolen*) *our money. His wife had gone off with the postman.* **3** *vt fus* (*inf*) to begin to dislike (someone or something once liked): *I've gone off Shakespeare. I went off that girl when I met her friends.* **4** *vi* to take place and be successful: *Did the party go off all right last night?* **5** *vi* (of an alarm) to ring, make a noise *etc*: *The thieves ran away as soon as the alarm went off.*

go on 1 *vi* (*often with* **to**) to continue going; to go as far as (a place): *There's no room in this hotel — let's go on to the next town.* **2** *vi* (*often with* **with**) to continue doing (something): *Go on with what you're doing.* **3** *vi* to continue (by doing something) after doing something: *The pianist played a piece by Bach, and then went on to play one of Beethoven's sonatas.* **4** *vi* to talk a great deal, usually too much, (about something): *She goes on and on about the time she met the Queen.* **5** *vi* (*inf*) to happen: *What is going on here?* **6** *vi* to pass by: *Things will get better as time goes on.* **7** *vi* to behave, especially badly: *If you go on like that much longer, someone will slap your face.* **8** *vt fus* to (be able to) base one's investigations *etc* on (information *etc*): *The police began a search for the murderer, but they had very few clues to go on.*

go on at *vt fus* (*inf*) to speak (to someone) in an angry or criticizing way, usually for some time: *Her mother went on at her for coming home late after the dance.*

go out *vi* **1** (*with* **to**) to go to a distant country, sometimes to stay: *I can't find a job here, so I'm going out to Canada to try there.* **2** to go to parties, meetings *etc*: *We don't go out as much as we did when we were younger.* **3** (*often with* **with**) to be seen frequently in the company of (a person, usually of the opposite sex): *My girl-friend* *and I have been going out (together) for eighteen months now.* **4** no longer to be part (of a competition *etc*) because one has been beaten: *The local team went out in the first round.*

go over 1 *vt fus* to study or look at (something) carefully: *I want to go over the work you have done before you do any more. The police went over the whole room for clues.* **2** *vt fus* to repeat (a story *etc*); to practise (part of a play, music *etc*): *Some of you haven't understood this lesson, so I'll go over the whole thing again. Act III is not very good yet, so we'll go over it again tomorrow. Act III is not very good, so I'll go over it again with you tomorrow.* **3** *vt fus* to list, discuss or consider: *I have no intention of going over all your faults.* **4** *vi (with* **to***)* to change to another religion, political party, type of food *etc*: *He's gone over to Christianity. I don't eat butter now — I've gone over to margarine.* **5** *vi* (of plays, behaviour *etc*) to be received (well or badly): *The play didn't go over at all well the first night.*

go through 1 *vt fus* to make a close study or examination of (something); to search for something in (something): *The treasurer went through the society's accounts. I've gone through all my pockets but I still can't find my key.* **2** *vt fus* to suffer: *You have no idea what I went through to get this finished in time.* **3** *vt fus* to use up (something): *He's gone through a lot of paper since he started.* **4** *vt fus* to do or complete (some action, ceremony *etc*): *You have to go through certain formalities before you can emigrate.* **5** *vi* to be agreed to or completed: *The Bill went through (* = was passed by Parliament*) yesterday. After long hours of negotiations, the deal went through.*

go through with *vt fus* to do (something) or finish doing (something): *I'm going to go through with this in spite of what you say. She went through with the wedding despite her parents' disapproval.*

go together *vi* **1** to look well together: *The carpet and curtains go together very well.* **2** (*inf*) (of a boy and girl) to have a close friendly relationship and be seen frequently together: *They have been going together for a year now.*

go towards *vt fus* to help to buy *etc* (something): *The money we collected will go towards a new roof for the church.*

go under *vi* to be ruined: *He has no idea how to run a shop — his business is bound to go under eventually.*

go up *vi* **1** to increase in size, value *etc*: *The temperature has gone up. The price of bread is going up tomorrow. He has gone up in my estimation* (= I think more highly of him than before). **2** to be built: *There are office blocks going up all over town.*

go with *vt fus* **1** to be given or sold with (something): *The carpets will go with the house.* **2** to look, taste *etc* well with (something): *The carpet goes with the wallpaper. Whisky doesn't go very well with tea.* **3** to be found in the same place as (something): *Illness often goes with poverty.* **4** to go steady with (someone): *I've been going with Mary for six months.*

go without *vi, vt fus* to manage without (something): *If you can't afford a new dress, you'll have to go without (one).*

gouge out *vt sep* **1** to make (a groove or hole) in something with a gouge or some other tool: *He gouged out a hole in the wood.* **2** to take, force or cut (a thing) out of something: *The tyrant gouged out the prisoner's eyes.*

grab at *vt fus* **1** to try to grasp or seize (a person, thing *etc*), not necessarily successfully: *He grabbed at the boy.* **2** (*fig*) to seize or take: *He grabbed at the chance to leave.*

grapple with *vt fus* **1** to grasp and fight (with a person *etc*): *The policeman grappled with the thief.* **2** (*fig*) to (try to) deal with (a problem *etc*), usually with some difficulty: *He enjoys grappling with mathematical problems.*

grasp at *vt fus* **1** to attempt to take hold of (a person, thing *etc*): *The drowning man grasped at a branch.* **2** (*fig*) to accept (an opportunity *etc*) eagerly: *I'd grasp at any opportunity to see France again.*

grate on / (*formal*) **upon** *vt fus* to irritate or annoy (someone): *His voice really grates on me.*

grind down *vt sep* (*usually fig*) to crush: *In spite of their brave resistance, the dictator finally ground them down by his constant tyranny. The people were ground down by heavy taxes. She was ground down by poverty.*

grind out *vt sep* (*inf*) to (continue to) to produce (something) over a period of time, often badly: *He was grinding out a tune. He was grinding out statements of his party's political doctrine.*

grind up *vt sep* to grind (something) into powder or small pieces: *This machine grinds up these rocks into powder. It grinds them up quickly.*

group together *vi, vt sep* to form into a group or groups: *We should group together all the books by the same author. Group these books together. Dictionaries and encyclopedias can be grouped together under the heading of reference books.*

grow into *vt fus* to become big enough to wear (clothes etc): *These shoes are a little too big for him, but he'll grow into them.*

grow on / (*formal*) **upon** *vt fus* to gradually become liked by (someone): *I didn't like the painting at first, but it has grown on me.*

grow out of *vt fus* **1** to become too big to wear (clothes etc): *He has grown out of that coat.* **2** to stop doing (something) as one grows older and becomes an adult: *He'll eventually grow out of sucking his thumb.*

grow up *vi* **1** to become an adult: *I'm going to be an engine-driver when I grow up.* **2** to behave the way an adult ought to behave: *I do wish he would grow up and stop behaving like a five-year-old.*

grub out / **up** *vt sep* to find or remove (something) by digging: *That stupid dog has grubbed up my prize roses.*

guard against *vt fus* (*formal*) to try to prevent (something) by being careful: *Check your work thoroughly in order to guard against mistakes.*

gun down *vt sep* to shoot or kill (a person) with a gun in a cruel or ruthless manner: *The bandits gunned down the villagers.*

gun for *vt fus (fig)* to attack or criticize (a person): *He has been gunning for me ever since I criticized his new book.*

H

hack at *vt fus* to hit (a tree *etc*) with something sharp (*eg* an axe): *He hacked at the trunk of the tree.*

hack down *vt sep* to cut (a tree *etc*) down with rough blows (*eg* of an axe).

hail from *vt fus (inf)* to come from or belong to (a place): *He hails from Texas.*

hammer away at *vt fus (inf)* to keep working on (a problem *etc*): *We'll hammer away at this until we get it solved.*

hammer out *vt sep* to produce (an agreement *etc*) with a great deal of effort and discussion: *The two political parties finally hammered out a solution which was acceptable to both of them.*

hand down *vt sep* to pass on (a precious object, a belief, a tradition *etc*) from one generation to the next: *These customs have been handed down from father to son since the Middle Ages. One generation handed them down to another.*

hand in *vt sep* **1** to give or bring (something) to a person, place *etc*: *The teacher told the children to hand in their exercise-books. They handed them in.* **2** to give or bring (something) to a person, place *etc* by coming or going into a place: *I'll hand this letter in to his office as I go past tonight. I'll also hand in the parcel.*

hand on *vt sep* to give (something) to someone: *When you have finished reading these notes, hand them on to the* person after you on the list. *The secret has been handed on from father to son.*

hand out *vt sep* **1** to give (a number of things) by hand (to several people): *The teacher handed out the books to all the pupils. They were handing out leaflets in the street.* **2** *(fig)* to give (something to someone): *It's very easy to hand out criticism, but could you do the job any better?*

hand over *vt sep* to give, send *etc* (a person, thing *etc* to someone): *We know you have the jewels, so hand them over. They handed the thief over to the police. (fig) The reporter handed the viewers over to Fred Smith in the television studio.*

hang about/around **1** *vi, vt fus (derog)* to stand around doing nothing: *I don't like to see all these youths hanging about (street-corners).* **2** *vt fus* to be close to (a person) frequently: *I don't want you hanging about my daughter.*

hang back *vi* to hesitate or be unwilling to do (something): *The soldiers all hung back when the sergeant asked for volunteers for the mission.*

hang on *vi* **1** to wait: *Will you hang on a minute — I'm not quite ready.* **2** *(often with* to*)* to hold (something): *Hang on to that rope.*

hang out **1** *vi (sl)* to live: *Where does he hang out nowadays?* **2** *vt sep* to hang (wet clothes *etc*) on a rope outside to dry: *I'll go and hang out the washing.*

hang together *vi (fig)* to agree or be consistent: *His statements just do not hang together — he must be lying.*

hang up **1** *vt sep* to hang (something) on something: *Hang up your coat in the cupboard. I'll hang the washing up in the bathroom.* **2** *vi (often with* on*)* to put the receiver back after a telephone conversation: *I tried to talk to her, but she hung up (on me).*

hanker after/for *vt fus (inf)* to want (something): *I rather hanker after going to America. She was obviously hankering for an invitation.*

happen on/upon *vt fus (formal)* to find (a person, thing) by chance: *He happened upon the perfect solution to the problem just as he was about to give up his research.*

hark back *vi (with* **to***) (formal)* to refer to something that has been said or done earlier: *Harking back to what you said last night, I think a decision will need to be made soon. To hark back to what you said, I think we should make a decision soon.*

harp on *vi, vt fus (inf)* to keep on talking or to talk too much (about something): *He's forever harping on (about his low wages). She keeps harping on his faults.*

have on 1 *vt sep* to wear: *That's a nice suit you have on.* **2** *vt oblig sep* to fool (someone): *You're having me on — that's not really true, is it?* **3** *vt oblig sep* to be busy with (something): *Have you anything on this afternoon?*

have up *vt sep (often in passive: usually with* **for***)* to make (a person) appear in court to answer some charge: *He was had up for drunken driving.*

head off 1 *vt sep* to make (a person, animal *etc*) change his, its *etc* direction of movement by getting in front of him, it *etc*: *One group of the soldiers rode across the valley to head the bandits off.* **2** *vi (inf)* to go in some direction: *He headed off towards the river.*

hear about/from/of *vt fus* to know (someone or something); to receive (news *etc*) about or from (someone or something): *'Have you heard from your sister?' I've never heard of him. Who is he? This is the first I've heard about moving to London.*

hear out *vt oblig sep (formal)* to allow (someone) to finish saying what he wants to say: *Please hear me out before you come to a decision.*

help out *vi, vt usually sep (inf)* to help (a person), usually for a short time because the person is in some difficulty: *I don't mind helping out in the shop from time to time, but not every day. Could you help me out by looking after the baby for an hour?*

hem in *vt sep* **1** to surround (someone): *The soldiers were hemmed in on all sides by the enemy.* **2** *(fig)* to make unable to move freely: *I feel hemmed in in the city.*

hinge on/*(formal)* **upon** *vt fus* to depend on: *The result of* *the whole competition hinges on the last match. Whether we go to France or not hinges on the cost of transport.*

hit back 1 *vt oblig sep* to hit (someone by whom one has been hit): *He hit me, so I hit him back.* **2** *vi (often with* **at***)* to criticize or attack in words (someone by whom one has been criticized or attacked): *He hit back at those who sneered at his plan.*

hit on/*(formal)* **upon** *vt fus* to find (an answer *etc*) by chance: *We've hit on the solution at last.*

hit out *vi (often with* **against** *or* **at***)* **1** to attempt to hit (someone): *The injured man hit out blindly at his attackers.* **2** to criticize or attack in words (someone with whom one does not agree): *The Prime Minister hit out at his opponents.*

hitch up *vt sep* to pull up or raise (something) with a sudden short pull: *He hitched up his trousers.*

hive off *vt sep* **1** to give (some work, part of a job *etc*) to some other person, firm *etc*: *If we can't meet the schedule, we can hive off some of the work to another firm.* **2** to make (part of an organization) independent: *We can hive off part of the company and make it a separate firm.*

hold back 1 *vt sep* to refuse to tell someone (something): *The police were convinced the man was holding something back.* **2** *vt sep* to prevent (something) from happening, being seen *etc*, usually with some effort: *The little girl succeeded in holding back her tears.* **3** *vt usually sep* to prevent (a person *etc*) from making progress or to make his progress slower: *I meant to finish cleaning the house but the children have held me back all day.*

hold down *vt sep* to keep or be allowed to stay in (a job): *He is incapable of holding down a job.*

hold forth *vi (usually derog)* to talk or give one's opinions, often loudly, at great length and forcefully or dogmatically: *The Prime Minister held forth for hours on the success of his government.*

hold off 1 *vi* (of weather) to stay away: *I hope the rain holds off.* **2** *vt sep* to keep (someone) away; to fight successfully against (an enemy attack): *The soldiers were greatly outnumbered but still managed to hold off the enemy.*

hold on *vi* **1** *(often with* **to***)* to keep (a grip on) (something): *She held on to me to stop herself slipping. Hold on to that rope and we'll pull you out. I couldn't hold on any longer, so I let go of the rope. Can I hold on to this book for another week?* **2** *(inf)* to stop or wait: *Hold on — I'm not quite ready yet. The telephonist asked the caller to hold on while she connected him with the manager's office.*

hold out 1 *vi* to continue to survive or resist difficulties, dangers *etc* until help *etc* arrives: *The rescue team hoped the people in the boat could hold out till they arrived.* **2** *vi* to continue to fight against an enemy attack: *The soldiers held out for eight days.* **3** *vi* to be enough to last: *Will our supplies hold out till the end of the month?* **4** *vt sep* to offer: *The doctor said he could hold out little hope for the patient.* **5** *vi* *(with* **for***)* to continue to demand or fight (for something): *The management offered the workers a rise of eight per cent, but the unions said they would hold out for fifteen per cent.*

hold out on *vt fus (inf)* to keep back money, information *etc* from (someone): *He says he knows nothing about it, but I think he's holding out on us.*

hold to *vt fus (formal)* to continue to believe, follow *etc* (opinions, decisions *etc*): *I've tried to tell him he's wrong, but he still holds to his original opinion.*

hold up *vt sep* **1** to stop or slow (the progress of something): *I'm sorry I'm late — I got held up at the office.* **2** to stop and rob (someone): *The bandits held up the stagecoach.* **3** *(with* **as***)* to show or mention (someone): *He was held up as an example to everyone.*

hold with *vt fus* to approve of (something): *He doesn't hold with smoking.*

hole out *vi* to hit a golf ball into a hole: *He holed out in one at the fourth hole* (= *He hit the golf ball from the tee into the hole with one stroke*).

hollow out *vt sep* **1** to make (something) hollow: *They hollowed out a tree-trunk to make a boat.* **2** to make (something) by making (something) hollow: *They hollowed out a boat.*

huddle up *vi (often with* **together***)* to huddle: *The cows huddled up together to keep warm.*

hunt down *vt sep* to search for (someone or something) until found: *The police hunted down the escaped prisoner.*

hunt for *vt fus (inf)* to search for: *I've been hunting for that shoe all morning.*

hunt out *vt sep (inf)* to search for (something that has been put away) until it is found: *I haven't got all the information you need with me, but I'll hunt it out for you. We should hunt out all our old clothes and give them to charity.*

hunt up *vt sep (inf)* to find or get (information *etc*) by study or research: *I'll hunt up the details for you in our library.*

hurry up 1 *vi, vt usually sep* to (cause to) move quickly: *Hurry him up, will you. Do hurry up!* **2** *vi (often with* **to***)* to come near quickly: *The woman hurried up to her husband.*

hush up *vt sep* to prevent (something) becoming known to the general public: *Their affair was hushed up to prevent a scandal.*

I

ice over/up *vi* to become covered with ice: *The garden pond iced over during the night. The car windows have iced up.*

identify with *vt fus* to feel sympathy for (someone) *eg* because he appears to have the same problems, feelings *etc* as one has: *When reading a novel, we very often identify with the main character in it.*

idle away *vt sep* to spend (time) doing nothing: *He is just idling the hours away.*

impinge on/upon *vt fus (formal)* **1** to interfere with (a person's freedom, rights *etc*): *The shade from the tree impinged on the adjoining garden.* **2** to come into contact with or make an impression on (a person's mind *etc*): *The sound impinged upon her ears.*

impress on/(formal) upon *vt* to stress (something or someone): *I must impress upon you the need for silence.*

improve on/(formal) upon *vt fus* to produce something which is better, more useful *etc* than (something else): *I think I can improve on that suggestion.*

indulge in *vt fus* to allow oneself to do (something) or to express (an emotion) not because one should but because one wishes to: *She indulged in a fit of temper. He tends to indulge in pessimism.*

inform against/on *vt fus (formal)* to tell facts to *eg* the police about (a criminal *etc*): *He informed against his fellow thieves.*

inquire about *vt fus* to ask for information about (something): *They inquired about trains to London.*

inquire after *vt fus* to ask for information about the state of (*eg* a person's health): *He inquired after her mother.*

inquire for *vt fus* **1** to ask to see or talk to (a person): *Someone rang up inquiring for you, but you were out.* **2** to ask for (goods in a shop *etc*): *Several people have been inquiring for the new catalogue.*

inquire into *vt fus* to try to discover the facts of: *The police are inquiring into the matter.*

interfere with *vt fus* to prevent, stop or slow down the progress of (something): *He doesn't let anything interfere with his game of golf on Saturday mornings.*

iron out *vt sep* **1** to get rid of (creases *etc*) by ironing: *I shall have to iron out the creases in this dress. Look at the creases in that skirt! Have you time to iron them out?* **2** (*fig*) to get rid of (difficulties *etc*) so that progress becomes easier: *They ironed out all the obvious problems at the first committee meeting. A few difficulties remain but I think we can iron them all out.*

J

jab at *vt fus* to poke or prod (at): *He jabbed at the tree angrily with his stick.*

jack up *vt sep* to raise (a motor car *etc*) and keep it supported, with a jack: *You need to jack up the car before you try to remove the wheel.*

jam on *vt sep* to put (brakes *etc*) on with force and haste: *When the dog ran in front of his car he jammed on his brakes and skidded. He jammed them on suddenly.*

jazz up *vt sep (inf)* to make (something, originally music) more lively or interesting: *He jazzed up the folk tune. I'll jazz up the stew with some courgettes. This party is boring — let's try and jazz it up a bit.*

join in 1 *vi* to take part: *We're playing a game — do join in!* **2** *vt fus* to take part in: *He would not join in the game/the conversation.*

join on *vi* to add oneself to a group: *They were going for a walk and we joined on.*

join up *vi* to become a member of an armed force: *He joined up in 1940.*

jolly along *vt usually sep (inf)* to keep (someone) in a good temper in order to gain his goodwill or co-operation: *He might help you, if you jolly him along a bit.*

jump at *vt fus (inf)* to take or accept eagerly: *He jumped at the chance to go to Germany for a fortnight.*

jump on *vt fus* **1** to make a sudden attack on: *He was waiting round the corner and jumped on me in the dark.* **2** *(inf fig)* to criticize unfairly: *She's always jumping on me for my bad spelling.*

K

keel over 1 *vt oblig sep* to turn (especially a boat) over: *He keeled the boat over to examine the hole made by the rock.* **2** *vi* to fall over (usually suddenly or unexpectedly): *She seemed to be perfectly well, and then she just keeled over in the middle of the kitchen.*

keep away *vi, vt sep* to (make something) remain at a distance: *Keep away — it's dangerous! She kept her children away until he had left.*

keep back 1 *vi, vt sep* not to (allow to) move forward: *She kept the child back on the edge of the crowd. Everybody keep back from the door! While his friends went up into the next class, John was kept back* (= was made to remain in his previous class). **2** *vt sep* not to tell or make known: *I feel he's keeping the real story back for some reason.* **3** *vt sep* not to give or pay out: *Part of my allowance is kept back to pay for my meals. Will they keep it back every week?*

keep down 1 *vi, vt sep* not to (allow to) rise up: *Keep down — they're firing at us!* (fig) *He won't let his mother keep him down any longer.* **2** *vt sep* to control or put a limit on: *They are taking steps to keep down the rabbit population. They won't keep it down for long.* **3** *vt sep* to digest without vomiting: *The patient is unable to keep down anything but water. He has eaten some food but he won't be able to keep it down.*

keep from *vt fus* to stop oneself from (doing something): *I could hardly keep from hitting him.*

keep in *vt usually sep* not to allow to go or come out or outside: *He's not well, so his mother has kept him in until he's better.*

keep in with *vt fus (inf)* to remain friendly with, usually for a special reason: *It's a good idea to keep in with the police in case you need their help one day.*

keep off 1 *vi, vt fus* to stay away (from): *There are notices everywhere warning people to keep off. The rain kept off and we had sunshine for the wedding. We kept off (= we did not speak about) the subject of money.* **2** *vt sep* to prevent (someone or something) from getting to or on to (something): *This umbrella isn't pretty, but it keeps off the rain. She tried in vain to keep the children off (the rose-bed). She could not keep them off (it).*

keep on 1 *vi* to continue (doing something or moving): *She kept on until it was finished. He didn't answer, but just kept on writing. They kept on until they came to a petrol station.* **2** *vt sep* to continue to use or employ: *We kept on the housekeeper after Grandfather died.*

keep on at *vt fus (inf)* to urge constantly (to do something): *She kept on at me to write to him.*

keep out 1 *vt sep* not to allow to enter: *This coat keeps out the wind. It does not keep it out completely.* **2** *vi* not to enter: *Keep out! This office is private.*

keep out of *vt fus (fig)* not to become involved in: *I tried to keep out of the argument as it was none of my business. Do try to keep out of trouble!*

keep to *vt fus* not to leave or go away from: *Keep to this side of the park! We kept to the roads we knew.*

keep up 1 *vt sep* to continue, or cause to remain, in operation: *I enjoy our friendship and try to keep it up. We try to keep up our family's reputation for hospitality. We do not always succeed in keeping it up.* **2** *vi, vt sep* to (cause to) remain in good condition: *He was finding it difficult to keep up the garden. He cannot keep it up properly. The weather has kept up well, hasn't it?* **3** *vi (often with* **with***)* to move fast enough not to be left behind (by): *Even the children managed to keep up. Don't run — I can't keep up with you. (fig) Everyone in the class was so clever that I couldn't keep up with them.*

kick about/around *(inf)* **1** *vt oblig sep* to treat badly or

bully: *The bigger boys are always kicking him around.*
2 *vi* to be lying *etc* without being used or dealt with:
*That letter has been kicking around for weeks and no-
one has answered it yet.* **3** *vi* to wander about without
having anything to do: *There was nothing going on, so
we kicked about a bit and then went home.*

kick off *vi* to start a football game by kicking the ball: *We
kick off at 2.30. (inf fig) I'll speak last at today's meeting
if you kick off (* = begin).

kick up *vt sep (inf)* to cause or start off (a row *etc*):
He kicked up a fuss about the mess in the garden.

kill off *vt sep* to destroy completely: *So many deer have
been shot that the species has almost been killed off. We
have killed them all off. (fig) I think that plan's been
killed off.*

kit out *vt sep (inf)* to provide with all the clothes, tools
etc necessary for a particular purpose: *He spent a lot
of money kitting himself out to go climbing in the
Antarctic. The old man kitted out the entire school
football team.*

kneel down *vi* to go into a kneeling position: *She knelt
down to look under the table.*

knock about/around *(inf)* **1** *vt oblig sep* to treat in a rough
and unkind manner, especially to hit repeatedly: *I've
heard that her husband knocks her about.* **2** *vi, vt fus*
to move about (in) in a casual manner without a definite
destination or purpose: *He spent six months knocking
around (in) Europe seeing the sights and living as
cheaply as possible.* **3** *vi* to be present without doing
anything in particular: *Three youths were knocking
around outside the cinema when the incident occurred.*

knock around/about with *vt fus (inf)* to be friendly with
or form part of the same group for social activities as:
*I don't like the people she knocks around with and I
wish she'd make some more friends of her own age.*

knock back *vt sep (inf)* to eat or drink, especially quickly
and/or in large quantities: *He knocked back three pints
of beer in the space of ten minutes.*

knock down *vt sep* 1 (especially of a person or a vehicle) to cause to fall by striking: *He was so angry with the man that he knocked him down. The old lady was knocked down as she crossed the street.* 2 *(inf)* to reduce the price of (goods): *She bought a coat that had been knocked down to half-price.* 3 *(with* **to***)* to sell (goods) at an auction: *The clock was finally knocked down to a dealer for $1000.*

knock off 1 *vt sep* to cause to fall off by striking: *He knocked her hat off with his umbrella.* 2 *vi, vt fus (inf)* to stop (working): *I knocked off (studying) at six o'clock after I had been working for four hours. What time do you knock off in this factory?* 3 *vt sep (sl)* to steal: *He was caught trying to get rid of a lot of cigarettes he had knocked off from a local tobacconist's. Where did you get that car? Did you knock it off?* 4 *vt sep (inf)* to reduce the price of something by a certain amount: *Since it was damaged, the shopkeeper knocked $2 off (the price). He refused to knock off any more.* 5 *vt sep (inf)* to complete or do hurriedly: *The typist knocked off all the letters before lunch. She knocked them all off.* 6 *vt sep (sl)* to kill: *The boys boasted that they had knocked off the old man. Run — I think you've knocked him off!*

knock out *vt sep* 1 to remove from position by striking: *He took a hammer and knocked out the peg. He knocked it out.* 2 to empty by a blow: *He knocked his pipe out on the ashtray.* 3 to make unconscious by a blow, or (in boxing) unable to recover within the required time: *The boxer knocked his opponent out in the third round. (fig) Those sleeping pills really knock you out. (fig) A bottle of these pills would knock out the whole family.* 4 to defeat and cause to retire from a competition: *That team knocked us out of the contest in the semi-finals. They knocked out our other team as well.*

knock over *vt sep* to cause to fall from an upright position: *The dog knocked over a chair as it rushed past. He knocked it over.*

knock up *vt sep* **1** to put together or make hurriedly: *We had to have somewhere to put the books, so my husband knocked up a couple of shelves. He knocked it up in two hours.* **2** *(inf)* to awaken by knocking: *He asked the hotel porter to knock him up at six o'clock as he had a train to catch. Will he knock up the whole family?* **3** *(sl usually refl)* to exhaust or make very tired: *Don't work so hard or you'll knock yourself up!* **4** *(vulg sl)* to make pregnant.

knuckle down *vi (inf: often with* **to***)* to start working seriously (at): *I don't really want to start studying for my exams but I'll just have to knuckle down (to it).*

knuckle under *vi (inf)* to give in (to someone else): *When we have disagreements, it's always me who has to knuckle under and do what I'm told.*

L

lack for *vt fus (formal: usually in neg)* not to have enough: *In any case, they don't lack for money. The children lack for nothing although the parents are poorly dressed.*

land up *vi (inf)* to finish or come eventually to be (in a certain, usually the wrong, place or a certain, usually bad, condition): *He wanted to go to London, but got on the wrong train and landed up in Bristol. If you go on like that, you'll land up in jail.*

lap up *vt sep* **1** to drink by lapping: *The dog lapped up the water.* **2** *(fig derog)* to accept eagerly, uncritically and in large quantities: *He was unbelievably insincere in his flattery, but she just lapped it up.*

lark about/around *vi (inf)* to play about in a rough and usually noisy manner: *Several teenagers were larking about in the hall.*

lash out *vi* **1** *(often with* **at***)* to kick or hit out violently: *He lashed out with his foot and kicked his attacker on* the ankle. (fig) In his speech the Prime Minister lashed out at his opponents. **2** (inf) to spend money in large quantities: For our anniversary, we decided to lash out and have a really big party.

last out vi, vt sep to be or have enough to survive or continue to exist (until the end of): I hope the petrol lasts out until we reach a garage. They could only last out another week on the little food they had. The sick man was not expected to last out the night.

laugh at vt fus to make it obvious that one regards something or someone as humorous, ridiculous or deserving scorn: Everyone will laugh at me if I wear that dress! He was not sure that it was a good idea, but the others laughed at his fears.

launch forth vi (formal or liter) to begin something in a colourful or dramatic manner: She launched forth into a long tale about what she had been doing.

launch out vi to throw oneself freely into some new activity (often involving spending money): The firm has recently launched out into the field of fashion.

lay aside vt sep to put away or to one side, especially to be used or dealt with at a later time: She laid aside several boxes that might be of use, and threw the rest out. She laid them aside for later use.

lay by vt sep to put away for future use: She laid by a store of tinned vegetables to be used in emergencies.

lay down vt sep **1** to give up; to cease by one's own actions to have: They laid down their arms. (fig) After losing the battle, the general laid down his command. (fig) The soldiers laid down their lives in the cause of peace. **2** to order or instruct: The rule book lays down what should be done in such a case. The correct procedure has been laid down by the manager. **3** to store: My father laid down a good stock of wine which I am now drinking.

lay in vt sep to get and store a supply of: I've laid in an extra stock of drinks for Christmas. You've laid it in too early.

lay into *vt fus (inf)* to beat thoroughly: *He laid into his attacker with his walking-stick.*

lay off 1 *vt sep* to dismiss (employees) temporarily: *Because of a shortage of orders, the firm has laid off a quarter of its workforce. His employer laid him off last week.* **2** *vt fus, vi (inf)* to stop (doing something): *I told him to lay off following me or he'd be sorry! I'm fed up with hearing about it and I wish you'd lay off!* **3** *vt fus (inf)* to leave alone and not annoy, attack, mention *etc*: *Lay off the subject of money while he's here. Oh, will you lay off him for just a moment!*

lay on *vt sep* to provide (a supply of): *The dinner was laid on by the firm. They laid on huge quantities of drink for the party.*

lay out *vt sep* **1** to arrange over a wide area (especially according to a plan): *He was the architect who laid out the public gardens. He laid them out at the request of the council.* **2** to spread so as to be easily seen: *He laid out the contents of the box on the table.* **3** *(inf)* to knock unconscious: *The branch struck him on the head and laid him out. Such a blow would have laid out anyone.* **4** *(inf)* to spend (money): *They laid out a lot of money on their daughter's wedding.* **5** *(formal)* to prepare (a dead body) to be buried: *The undertaker has laid out the old lady.*

lay up *vt sep* **1** to keep or store: *We laid up a good supply of apples this year from our own trees. (fig) She's laying up problems for the future by her behaviour.* **2** to put (a ship) out of use in a dock: *The ship is laid up at Portsmouth being refitted.*

lead off *vi, vt sep* to begin: *The band led (the dance) off with a waltz.*

lead on 1 *vt oblig sep* to deceive by causing to have false hopes: *She led us on to believe that we would be paid for our work.* **2** *vi* to go forward first: *Lead on, then!*

lead up to *vt fus* to prepare (to do something, for something to happen *etc*) by steps or stages: *He talked for a long time and seemed to be leading up to something.*

lean on

We studied the events leading up to the First World War.

lean on *vt fus* **1** to use as a support: *The lame man leaned on a stick. (fig) She leans on her husband for advice.* **2** *(fig: sl)* to use slight force to persuade (someone) to do something *etc*: *I'll have to lean on her a bit — I don't think she's working hard enough.*

leave off *vi, vt fus (inf)* to stop (doing something): *You can leave off looking for the book — I've found it. I wish you would leave off!*

leave out *vt sep* not to include or put in: *You've left out a word in that sentence. We'll have to invite her because we can hardly leave her out.*

let down *vt sep* **1** to lower: *She let down the blind. She let it down slowly.* **2** to disappoint or fail to help when necessary *etc*: *You must give a film show at the party — you can't let the children down. She felt he had let her down by not coming.* **3** to make flat by allowing the air to escape: *When he came back, he found that some children had let his car tyres down. They had been let down some hours before.* **4** to make longer: *She had to let down the child's skirt.*

let in *vi* to allow water *etc* to pass in: *This pair of boots is letting in badly.*

let off *vt sep* **1** to fire (a gun) or cause (a firework *etc*) to explode: *He let the gun off in error. He let it off accidentally.* **2** to allow to go without punishment *etc*: *The policeman let him off with a warning. The police let off all the young offenders. I'll let you off (doing the washing up). The taxman let us off with half of what we expected to pay.*

let up *vi* to become less strong or violent; to stop: *I do wish the rain would let up. He never lets up, does he?*

level off *vi, vt sep* to make or become flat, even, steady *etc*: *She levelled off the icing on the cake with a knife. (fig) After rising for so long, prices have not levelled off.*

level out *vi, vt sep* to make or become level: *The road levels out as it comes down to the plain. We have been* *trying to level out differences in the price of our goods in various shops. We did not succeed in levelling them all out.*

lie back *vi* **1** to lean back on a support: *He lay back against the pillows and went to sleep.* **2** (*fig*) to rest, especially after a period of hard work: *I thought I'd just lie back and enjoy myself.*

lie down *vi* to take a flat or horizontal position: *The dog/ man lay down. I've just washed my hair, and I can't get it to lie down.*

lie in *vi* **1** to stay in bed late in the morning: *I like to lie in until nine on a Saturday.* **2** to be in bed before and after giving birth to a child.

lie with *vt fus* (*formal*) (of a choice, duty *etc*) to be the responsibility of: *The decision lies with you.*

lift off *vi* (of a rocket *etc*) to leave the ground.

light on *vt fus* to find by chance: *While wandering round the town, we lit on a very cheap restaurant.*

light up 1 *vi* to begin to give out light: *As we watched, the streetlights lit up.* **2** *vi, vt sep* to make, be or become full of light: *The powerful searchlight lit up the building. It lit them all up. She watched the house light up as everyone awoke.* **3** *vi, vt sep* (*fig*) to make or become happy: *Her face lit up when she saw him. When she smiles, it lights up her whole face. It lights it up completely.* **4** *vi* (*inf*) to light a cigarette *etc*: *He produced a cigar and lit up.*

limber up *vi* to exercise so as to become able to move easily: *The hall was full of dancers limbering up before the performance.*

line up 1 *vi, vt sep* to form a line (of): *The children lined up ready to leave the classroom. She lined up the chairs in front of the stage.* **2** *vt sep* (*inf*) to collect, prepare and arrange: *I have lined up several important people for you to meet. There are a lot of interesting programmes lined up to be shown on television this autumn.*

link up *vi, vt sep* to join or be joined closely or by a link: *This exercise links up with the work you were doing* *last week. An electrician called to link up our house to the mains electricity supply.*

listen in *vi* **1** (*often with* **to**) to listen to a radio broadcast: *If you listen in tonight you'll hear my brother talking about his new play.* **2** (*often with* **on**) to listen intentionally to a telephone conversation, a message intended for someone else *etc*: *It was impossible to discuss anything private over the telephone, as the operator was in the habit of listening in (on our conversations).*

live down *vt sep* to continue living in a normal way until a wrong action, mistake *etc* is forgotten: *It took her a long time to live down the scandal caused by her arrest. She never really lived it down.*

live in, out *vi* to have one's home at or away from the place where one works: *All the hotel staff live in. She chose to live out and to be paid extra.*

live on *vt fus* **1** to keep oneself alive by eating: *He lives on fish and potatoes.* **2** to be supported (financially) by: *He lives on $50 a week. (derog) She and her children live on the State.*

live up to *vt fus* to behave in a manner worthy of: *He found it difficult to live up to the reputation of being a hero.*

lock in *vt usually sep* to prevent from getting out of a building *etc* by using a lock: *She found someone had locked her in, and had to climb out of the window.*

lock out *vt usually sep* **1** to prevent from getting into a building *etc* by using a lock: *It is easy to lock yourself out (of the house) if you forget your key.* **2** to prevent (employees) from entering a factory *etc* during an industrial dispute: *The steelworkers have been locked out.*

lock up **1** *vt sep* to confine or prevent from leaving or being taken away by using a lock: *She locks up the silver in a safe after using it. She locked it up.* **2** *vi* to lock whatever should be locked: *He always locks up before leaving the shop in the evening.* **3** *vt sep* to lock very securely: *He locked up the front door and went to* *bed. He locked it up every night.*

look after *vt fus* to attend to or take care of: *She is paid to look after the children. The secretary looks after all the complaints we receive.*

look ahead *vi* (*often with* **to**) to consider what will happen at some time in the future: *Let's look ahead to next month and consider what to do then.*

look down on *vt fus* to think of (someone or something) as being inferior: *She has always looked down on us for not having a car.*

look for *vt fus* **1** to search for: *She lost her handbag and wasted ten minutes looking for it.* **2** to expect: *He is always looking for praise.*

look forward to *vt fus* to wait with pleasure for (something which is going to happen): *I am looking forward to seeing you. She is looking forward to the Christmas holidays.*

look in *vi* (*often with* **on**) to visit briefly and without invitation: *I decided to look in (on Paul and Carol) on my way home.*

look into *vt fus* to inspect or investigate closely: *I shall look into the possibility of buying a house. The manager is going to look into your complaint.*

look on **1** *vi* to watch something without taking part: *No, I don't want to play — I'd rather look on.* **2** *vt fus* (*with* **as**) to think of or consider: *I have lived with my aunt since I was a baby, and I look on her as my mother. She looked on his behaviour as a grave mistake.*

look out **1** *vi* (*usually with* **for**) to watch: *She was looking out for him and saw him long before he saw her.* **2** *vt sep* to find by searching or choose: *I've looked out a couple of books I think might be useful to you. I must look out my winter clothes if the weather's going to be cold.*

look over *vt fus, vt sep* to examine, but not with great care: *We have been looking over the new house. You have looked over it already. Have you looked over my notes? I've looked over them/looked them over.*

look through *vt fus* to look at or study (a book, papers *etc*), usually briefly: *I've looked through your report and made some notes on it.*

look up 1 *vi (inf)* to improve or become better: *Things have been looking up lately and most of my worries have disappeared.* **2** *vt sep (inf)* to pay a visit to (a person): *I hadn't seen them for months so I thought it was time I looked them up. We looked up several old friends.* **3** *vt sep* to search for in a book of reference: *You should look the word up (in a dictionary).* **4** *vt sep* to consult (a reference book): *I looked up the encyclopedia and it doesn't mention him. I looked it up twice.*

look up to *vt fus* to respect the conduct, opinions *etc* of: *He has always looked up to his father.*

lose out *vi* to suffer loss or be at a disadvantage: *She lost out by being ill and missing the party.*

lump together *vt sep* to treat or think of as (all) alike: *She lumped the whole family together in her mind as a group of idiots.*

lust after/for *vt fus (especially liter or facet)* to desire greatly: *He's always lusting after some woman. They lusted for revenge.*

M

make for *vt fus* **1** to go towards: *We're making for Glasgow, via York.* **2** *(formal)* to have as a result; to cause: *All these arguments make for bad feeling among the people involved.*

make off *vi (formal)* to go away, especially hurriedly or secretly: *They made off in the middle of the night.*

make off/away with *vt fus (formal)* to run away with or steal: *Thieves made off with all her jewellery.*

make out 1 *vt sep* to see, hear or understand: *Can you make out what he's trying to say? He could make out a* ship in the distance. *I cannot make it out.* **2** *vt fus* to make it seem (that): *He made out that he was earning a huge amount of money.* **3** *vt sep* to write or fill in: *The doctor made out a prescription. He made it out yesterday.* **4** *vi (inf)* to manage or succeed: *We'll make out, despite all these problems. How are you making out these days?*

make over *vt sep (formal)* to transfer (especially ownership): *The property was made over to the son before his father died.*

make up 1 *vt sep* to invent: *He made up the whole story — it's all lies. She's very good at making up stories to tell the children at bedtime. She made the whole thing up.* **2** *vt sep* to put together: *I'll make up a parcel and send it to you. She will help me make it up.* **3** *vt sep* to compose or be part(s) of: *Ten poems make up the entire book. The group was made up of doctors and lawyers.* **4** *vt sep* to complete: *We need one more player — will you make up the number(s)?* **5** *vi, vt sep* to apply cosmetics to (the face): *I don't like to see women making up (their faces) in public.* **6** *vi, vt sep* to become friends again (after a quarrel *etc*): *They've finally made up (their disagreement).*

make up for *vt fus* to supply a reward, substitute *etc* for (disappointment, damage, loss of money or time *etc*): *This will make up for all the occasions when you've lost. Next week we'll try to make up for lost time.*

make up to *vt fus (inf)* to try to gain the favour or love of (by flattery *etc*): *She's always making up to the teacher by bringing him presents.*

map out *vt sep* to plan (a route, course of action *etc*) in detail: *We started to map out a possible route for our journey. We did not have time to map it out in detail.*

mark down, up *vt sep* to bring down or increase the price of (an article for sale in a shop): *This jacket has been marked down from $10 to $8.*

mark off *vt sep* to put marks on (something) indicating divisions *etc*: *The artist marked off his canvas in* squares *before starting to paint. He marked it off neatly.*

mark out *vt sep* **1** to mark the boundary of (*eg* a football pitch) by making lines *etc*: *The pitch was marked out with white lines. They marked it out yesterday.* **2** to select or choose for some particular purpose *etc* in the future: *He had been marked out for an army career from early childhood.*

marry off *vt sep* (*inf*) to find a husband or wife for (one's son or daughter): *He managed to marry off all his daughters to wealthy or aristocratic young men. He has finally married her off.*

match up *vi, vt sep* to be, or make, similar in some way *eg* colour or pattern: *These two pieces of material don't match up very well.*

measure off *vt sep* to measure and mark *etc* (a given amount): *She took out the roll of cloth and measured off two metres.*

measure out *vt sep* to give (to someone) a measured amount of (something): *He measured (me) out a kilo of sugar. Is that the correct weight of sugar? Did he measure it out?*

measure up *vi* (*often with* **to**) to reach a certain (required) standard: *John's performance doesn't measure up (to the others/to our requirements).* **2** *vt sep* to find and take a note of the measurements of (a person): *The tailor measured him up for his new suit.*

melt down *vt sep* to melt (a metal object) so that it loses its shape: *He melted down the stolen silver articles into lumps of metal.*

mess about/around **1** *vi* (*inf*) to behave in a foolish or annoying way: *The children were shouting and messing about in the classroom when the teacher arrived.* **2** *vi* to work with no particular plan in a situation that involves mess: *I love messing about in the kitchen.* **3** *vi* (*with* **with**) to meddle or interfere with: *Who's been messing about with my papers?* **4** *vt usually sep* to upset or put into a state of disorder or confusion: *The travel agents* *have really messed me about. The wind messed her hairstyle about a bit.*

mess up *vt sep* to spoil; to make a mess of: *My husband's broken leg has really messed up our holiday plans. Don't mess the room up! You've messed it up already.*

mete out *vt sep* (*formal*) to give (punishment *etc*): *The judge meted out severe sentences to all the criminals.*

miss out 1 *vt sep* to omit or fail to include: *Don't miss out your brother when you send round the invitations.* **2** *vi* (*inf*) (*often with* **on**) to be left out (of something) or unable to take part (in) or enjoy (something): *George missed out (on all the fun) because of his broken leg.*

mist over *vi* to become covered (as if) with mist: *The hills misted over. The mirror misted over* (= became covered in condensation).

mist up 1 *vi* (of a surface) to mist over: *The mirror/ windscreen misted up.* **2** *vt sep* to cause (a surface) to mist over: *Their breath misted up the windows.*

mix up *vt sep* **1** to blend (different things) together: *Put the eggs and sugar in the bowl and mix them up together. I'll need to mix up another tin of paint.* **2** to confuse or muddle (different things): *I mixed the dates up and arrived on the wrong day. I'm always mixing the twins up. She put the lottery tickets in the hat and mixed them up thoroughly.* **3** to confuse or upset (a person): *You've mixed me up with all this information.*

monkey about/around *vi* (*often with* **with**: *inf*) to act foolishly; to interfere: *Stop monkeying around (with my papers)!*

moon about/around *vi* to wander around as if dazed, *eg* because one is in love: *Ever since she met that boy, she spends her time mooning around waiting for him to telephone.*

mop up *vt sep* to clean (something) away (using a mop, cloth, piece of paper *etc*): *He mopped up the mess with his handkerchief. (inf fig) The troops mopped up the remains of the enemy forces within a week.*

move along *vi, vt sep* to keep moving, not staying in one place: *The police told the crowd that had gathered to move along. They moved us along.*

move in *vi* to go into and occupy a house *etc*: *We can move in on Saturday. (fig) When his business collapsed, we moved in and took over all his old customers.*

move off *vi* (of vehicles *etc*) to begin moving away: *The bus moved off just as I got to the bus stop.*

move on *vi, vt sep* to (cause to) move to another place, situation *etc*: *The policeman moved the drunk man on. He tried to move him on. I feel like moving on and doing something different.*

move out *vi* to leave, and cease to live in, a house *etc*: *She has to move out before the new tenants arrive.*

move up *vi, vt sep* to move in any given direction so as to make more space: *Move up and let me sit down, please. If we moved all these chairs up a bit, there would be room for two more.*

mow down *vt sep* to kill (soldiers *etc*) in large numbers: *Our troops were mown down by machine-gun fire. The enemy troops mowed them down.*

muck about/around *vi* (*inf*) **1** to do things without a definite plan: *He is just mucking about in the garden.* **2** to act foolishly: *Stop mucking about!*

muck in *vi* (*inf*) to share *eg* accommodation, work *etc*: *I mucked in with Jim till I found a flat of my own. We all mucked in and finished the job in two days.*

muck out *vi, vt sep* (*inf*) to clean (especially stables): *It's her turn to muck out (the stable).*

muck up *vt sep* (*inf: especially fig*) to make a mess of: *You've mucked up the whole house with your dirty boots! (fig) You've mucked up my plans for the evening. You've mucked them up by asking him to join us.*

muddle along/through *vi* to progress in spite of one's unsatisfactory methods and foolish mistakes: *She is a very disorganized person but she always seems to muddle through.*

muddle up *vt usually sep* to confuse (*eg* two different things): *I'm always muddling the twins up.*

N

nail up *vt sep* to fasten or close completely with nails: *He tried to open the door, but it was nailed up.*

nip along/in(to)/out/over *vi, vt fus* to move quickly; to make a quick, usually short journey: *Why don't you nip along the road to the shops for a paper? I'll just nip into this shop for cigarettes. He nipped over to Paris for the weekend.*

nod off *vi (inf)* to fall asleep: *He nodded off while she was speaking to him.*

nose about/around *vi, vt fus* to look or search (in something) as if by smelling: *He nosed about (in) the cupboard.*

nose out *vt sep (inf)* to find (something) by smelling: *The dog nosed out its master's glove. (fig The detective nosed out a plot to rob the bank. They nosed it out quickly.*

notch up *vt sep (inf)* to achieve or score (something): *He has notched up more goals than anyone else this season. He notched them up in four matches.*

note down *vt sep* to write down: *He noted down what she said. He noted it all down.*

O

offend against *vt fus* to act wrongly according to law, usual customs, religious belief *etc*: *His behaviour offends against good manners. Such an action would offend against God.*

open on to *vt fus* (of a door *etc*) to open towards (a garden *etc*): *Our front door opens (straight) on to the street — we have no front garden.*

open out 1 *vt sep* to unfold or spread out (a map): *The hikers opened out the map to see which route they ought to take. They opened it out carefully.* **2** *vi* (of flowers) to become open: *The tulips are beginning to open out at last.*

open up 1 *vt sep* to open (a shop *etc*): *They've opened up a new bookshop in the High Street. I open up the shop at nine o'clock every morning. She opened it up yesterday.* **2** *vt sep* to open (a box *etc*) completely: *He opened up the parcel. He opened it up quickly.* **3** *vi* (*usually in imperative*) to open the (main) door of a building *etc*: *"Open up!" shouted the policeman. "We know you are in there!"*

opt out *vi* (*often with of*) to choose or decide not to do something or take part in something: *You promised to help us, so you can't opt out (of it) now.*

order about *vt usually sep* (*often derog*) to keep on giving orders (to someone): *I'm tired of him ordering me about all the time.*

own up *vi* (*often with to*) to admit that one has done something: *Who did this? Own up! He owned up to having broken the window.*

P

pace out *vt sep* to measure by walking along, across *etc* with even steps: *She paced out the room and decided that the carpet would fit.*

pack in (*inf*) **1** *vt sep* to abandon or stop doing, using *etc*: *It was so difficult I just packed in the whole idea. Pack that in, will you!* **2** *vi* to stop working or operating: *The engine has packed in.*

pack off *vt sep* (*inf*) to send away, usually quickly and without wasting time: *He packed off his children to do their homework. They packed the children off to bed early.*

pack up 1 *vt sep* to put into containers in order to take somewhere else: *She spent the weekend packing up the contents of her house.* **2** *vi (sl)* to stop working or operating: *We'd only gone five kilometres when the engine packed up. At one point the doctor thought her kidneys were packing up, but she's all right now.*

pad out *vt sep* to fill (something) with a soft material to make it the right size: *The actor's costume was padded out to make him look fat. (fig) He felt his letter was not long enough, so he padded it out with remarks about the weather.*

pair off *vi, vt sep* to join together with one other person to make a pair: *The boys and girls all paired off at the party. Their parents paired John and Mary off when they were children.*

pall on *vt fus (formal)* to become boring or uninteresting to (a person): *The little girl was reading, but the book had no pictures and soon palled on her.*

pander to *vt fus (derog)* to give (someone) something that he likes but which is morally wrong or bad: *Some newspapers pander to people's interest in crime and violence.*

part with *vt fus (inf)* to give away or be separated from: *He doesn't like parting with money.*

pass as/for *vt fus* to be mistaken for or accepted as: *Some man-made materials could pass as silk. His nasty remarks pass for wit among his admirers.*

pass away *vi (euph)* to die: *Her grandmother passed away last night.*

pass by 1 *vi, vt fus* to go past (a particular place): *I was passing by when the bride arrived at the church. She passed by the hospital on the way to the office.* **2** *vt oblig sep* to ignore or take no notice of: *They passed him by when the new jobs were given out.*

pass off *vi* **1** (sickness, an emotion *etc*) to go away: *By the evening, his sickness had passed off and he felt better.* **2** (of an event) to happen (with emphasis on the fact that the course of the event was not stopped or spoiled): *The wedding passed off very well in the end.*

pass on 1 *vt sep* to give to someone else (usually something which one has been given by a third person): *I passed on his message to Mrs Brown. Please read this note and pass it on.* **2** *vi (euph)* to die: *I am sorry to tell you that mother passed on yesterday.*

pass out 1 *vi* to faint: *I feel as though I'm going to pass out.* **2** *vi* to leave or graduate from a college, especially military or police. **3** *vt sep* to give to several different people: *The teacher passed out the books to her class.*

pass over 1 *vt fus* to ignore or overlook: *We'll pass over that remark.* **2** *vt oblig sep* to ignore, fail to consider (for a job *etc*): *This is the third time he's been passed over for that job. They passed him over for promotion.*

pass up *vt sep (inf)* not to accept (a chance, opportunity *etc*): *He passed up the offer of a good job in America to come here. He passed the job up without even considering it.*

patch up *vt sep* **1** to mend, especially quickly and temporarily: *He patched up the roof with bits of wood.* **2** *(fig)* to settle (a quarrel): *They soon patched up their disagreement. They patched it up yesterday.*

pay back *vt sep* **1** to give back (to someone something that one has borrowed): *I'll pay you the $5 back tomorrow. I'll pay you back as soon as I can.* **2** *(inf fig)* to punish, have revenge on: *I'll pay you back for that!*

pay off 1 *vt sep* to pay in full and discharge (workers) because they are no longer needed: *Hundreds of steelworkers have been paid off.* **2** *vi (fig)* to have good results: *His hard work paid off.*

pay out 1 *vi, vt sep* to spend or give (money), *eg* to pay bills, debts *etc*: *I'm not willing to pay out large sums of money to repair an old car like this. Her father is always paying out to settle her bills.* **2** *vt sep* to cause or allow (rope *etc*) to become slack.

pay up *vi, vt sep (inf)* to give (money) to someone, *eg* in order to pay a debt: *You lost the bet, so pay up (what you owe me). You have three days to pay up (= You must pay up within three days). Please pay it up.*

pension off *vt sep (sometimes derog)* to allow to retire, or to dismiss, with a pension: *They pensioned him off when they found a younger man for the job.*

perk up *vi, vt sep (inf)* to recover one's energy or cheerfulness: *I gave her a cup of tea and she soon perked up. A cup of tea will soon perk you up.*

phase in, out *vt sep* to begin or stop doing, using *etc* (something) in stages: *These new teaching methods will be gradually phased in and the old methods phased out.*

phone up *vi, vt sep* to (try to) speak to (someone) by means of the telephone: *If you have any problems, just phone me up. He has phoned up all the people concerned. I'll phone up and ask about it.*

pick at *vt fus* **1** to eat very little of (something): *He was not very hungry, and just picked at the food on his plate.* **2** to keep on touching, scratching or pulling at (something, especially a scab): *Do stop picking at that scab or the cut will never heal.*

pick off *vt sep* to shoot (especially people in a group) one by one: *He picked off the enemy soldiers as they tried to leave their hut.*

pick on *vt fus (inf)* **1** to choose (someone) to do a usually difficult or unpleasant job: *Why do they always pick on me to do the washing-up?* **2** to speak to or treat (a person) angrily or critically: *Don't pick on me because we didn't get this finished on time — it wasn't my fault.*

pick out *vt sep* **1** to choose or select: *She picked out one dress that she particularly liked.* **2** to see or recognize (a person, thing *etc*) in a crowd: *He must be among those people getting off the train, but I can't pick him out.* **3** to play (a piece of music), especially slowly and with difficulty, especially by ear, without music in front of one: *I don't really play the piano, but I can pick out a tune on one with one finger.*

pick up 1 *vt sep* to learn gradually, without formal teaching: *I never studied Italian — I just picked it up when I was in Italy.* **2** *vi, vt sep* to let (someone) into a car, train *etc* in order to take him somewhere: *I picked him up at* *the station and drove him home. The bus stopped at the end of the road to pick up passengers. The train only picks up at certain stations.* **3** *vt sep* to get (something) by chance: *I picked up a real bargain at the shops today. You can pick up quite a lot of gossip in a pub.* **4** *v refl sep* to stand up: *He fell over and picked himself up again.* **5** *vt sep (inf)* to collect (something) from somewhere: *I ordered some meat from the butcher — I'll pick it up on my way home.* **6** *vt sep* (of radio, radar *etc*) to receive signals: *We picked up a foreign broadcast last night.* **7** *vt sep* to find; to catch: *We lost his trail but picked it up again later. The police picked up the man they wanted outside the cinema.* **8** *vi (inf)* to recover (health): *He has been very ill, but he's picking up again now.* **9** *vt sep (sl)* (especially of a man) to form a casual, not permanent, and usually sexual, relationship with a person of the opposite sex: *He picked her up at a party last Saturday.*

piece together *vt sep* to put (the pieces of something) together: *They tried to piece together the fragments of the broken vase. (fig) We managed to piece together his story.*

pile up *vi, vt sep* to make or become a pile; to accumulate: *He piled up the earth at the end of the garden. The rubbish piled up in the kitchen. (fig) His debts soon piled up.*

pin down *vt oblig sep (fig)* to make (someone) give (a definite answer, statement, opinion or promise): *I can't pin him down to a definite date for his arrival. He refused to be pinned down about his opinions on abortion.*

pipe down *vi (inf)* to stop talking; to be quiet: *Will you pipe down for a moment?*

pipe up *vi (inf)* to say (something); to start speaking: *He soon piped up with a question.*

piss off *vi (vulg: usually as a command)* to go away: *Why don't you just piss off and leave me alone!*

pitch in *vi (inf)* to (begin to) deal with, do *etc* something:

If everyone pitches in, we'll soon get the job done. There's plenty of food for everyone, so pitch in.

pitch into *vt fus (inf)* **1** to attack; to start a fight or argument: *He pitched into her about her careless work.* **2** to (begin to) deal with, do *etc* (something): *Everyone pitched into the work/food.*

plan ahead *vi* to plan (something) a (fairly) long time before it will happen *etc*: *If you want to be successful in publishing, you have to plan ahead.*

play at *vt fus* **1** to pretend to do or be (something); to do (something) in a not serious way: *The children were playing at cowboys and Indians. He only plays at being a poet — he never actually writes any poetry.* **2** *(inf)* (used especially when questioning angrily why someone is doing something) to do: *What does he think he's playing at?*

play back *vt sep* to play (music, speech *etc*) on a record or tape after it has just been recorded: *They recorded the song and then played it back to the singer.*

play down *vt sep* to try to make (something) appear less important: *He played down the fact that he had failed the exam.*

play on/*(formal)* **upon** *vt fus* to make use of (someone's feelings, fears *etc*): *He played on my sympathy until I lent him $50.*

play up *vi* **1** *(inf)* to be troublesome or disobedient: *The children are playing up today.* **2** *(with* **to***)* to flatter or pretend to admire (someone) for one's own advantage: *He is always playing up to the manager.*

plead with *vt fus* to make an urgent request: *He pleaded with me not to go.*

plough back *vt sep* to put (money, profits *etc*) back (into a business *etc*): *He made a profit last year, but ploughed it back so that he could buy more machinery.*

plough through *vt fus* to travel with difficulty, force a way *etc*: *The ship ploughed through the rough sea. (fig) I've been ploughing through a very dull book.*

plug away *vi (inf) (often with* **at***)* to work very hard (at):

plug in

He is plugging away (at his studies) every evening.

plug in vi, vt sep to connect up (an electrical apparatus), or be connected up, by inserting its mains plug into a socket: Could you plug in the electric kettle, please? The kettle plugs in over there.

plump down 1 vi to sit or fall down heavily: She plumped down on the sofa. **2** vt sep to put down heavily: He plumped his books down on the table.

plump for vt fus (inf) to choose or decide on: She finally plumped for a house in the country.

plump up vt sep to shake out (cushions etc): The nurse plumped up his pillows to make him comfortable.

point out vt sep to indicate or draw attention to: He pointed out his house to her. I pointed out (= drew attention to the fact) that we needed more money.

poke about/around vi (inf) to look or search for something among other things: He was poking about in the attic. He poked around for his pen in my desk.

polish off vt sep (inf) to finish: She polished off the last of the food.

pop up vi (inf) to appear: I never know where he'll pop up next.

pore over vt fus to study with great attention: He pored over his books.

portion out vt sep (formal) to divide into portions or shares: The money was portioned out between the three children.

pounce on vt fus to leap upon (eg one's prey) in order to attack or grab it: The tiger pounced on its victim. (fig) He pounced on the book he had been looking for. (fig) She pounced on the weak point in his argument.

preside at/over vt fus (formal or facet) to be the chairman of (a meeting etc): The Prime Minister presided at/over the meeting. (fig) Grandmother presided at the dinner table.

press for vt fus to try to get; to keep demanding: The miners are pressing for higher wages.

press forward/on vi to continue (in spite of difficulties):

They pressed forward through the crowd. She pressed on with her work.

presume on *vt fus* to take advantage of; to make use of in an unjustified way: *He is presuming on your good nature.*

prevail on/upon *vt fus (formal)* to persuade: *Can I prevail on you to stay for supper?*

prey on/upon *vt fus (formal)* to attack as prey: *Hawks prey upon smaller birds. (fig) Fears preyed on her mind.*

proceed against *vt fus (legal)* to take legal action against: *The police decided not to proceed against her.*

proceed from *vt fus (formal)* to be the result of; to originate in: *Fear often proceeds from ignorance.*

profit from/by *vt fus* to gain profit(s) from: *The business profited from its exports. I am profiting by my mistakes.*

pry into *vt fus (derog)* to try to find out about (something secret, especially other people's affairs): *He is always prying into my business.*

puff out *vt sep* to cause to swell or expand: *The bird puffed out its feathers. He puffed out his cheeks.*

puff up *vi (inf)* to swell: *Her eye puffed up after the wasp stung her.*

pull down *vt sep* to destroy or demolish (buildings): *They pulled down the old shop and built a supermarket. They pulled it down last year.*

pull off *vt sep (inf)* to succeed in doing (something): *He's finally pulled it off! He's pulled off a good business deal.*

pull on *vt sep* to put on (a piece of clothing) hastily: *She pulled on a sweater. He pulled on his shoes. He pulled them on hurriedly.*

pull through *vi, vt sep (inf)* to (help to) survive an illness etc: *He is very ill, but he'll pull through.*

pull up *vi* (of a driver or vehicle) to stop: *He pulled up at the traffic lights.*

pump up *vt sep* to inflate (tyres *etc*) with a pump.

push along *vi (inf)* to leave or go away: *I'll have to be pushing along now.*

push around *vt oblig sep (inf)* to treat (someone) roughly: *He pushes his younger brother around. (fig) I don't let anyone push me around.*

push off *vi (inf)* to go away: *I wish you'd push off!*

push on *vi (inf)* to go on; to continue: *I'm late, I'll have to push on. Push on with your work.*

push over *vt sep* to cause to fall; to knock down: *He pushed me over.*

put about 1 *vt sep (formal)* to spread (news *etc*): *They put (it) about that she was married.* **2** *vi (nautical)* to change direction: *They put about and sailed for home.*

put across/over *vt sep* to convey or communicate (ideas *etc*) to others: *He's very good at putting his ideas across. He has a great deal of information but he does not put it across very well.*

put aside *vt sep* **1** to abandon (work *etc*) temporarily: *She put aside her needlework. She put it aside.* **2** to save or preserve for the future: *He tries to put aside a little money each month.*

put away *vt sep* to return (something) to its proper place, especially out of sight: *She put her clothes away in the dresser. She put them away.*

put back *vt sep* to return (something) to its proper place: *Did you put my keys back?*

put by *vt sep* to save or preserve for the future: *I have put by some money (for emergencies).*

put down *vt sep* **1** to lower (one's hand *etc*): *The teacher asked the pupil to put his hand down.* **2** to place on the floor or other surface, out of one's hands: *Put that knife down immediately!* **3** *(formal)* to subdue (a rebellion *etc*): *The revolt was quickly put down.* **4** *(inf)* to humiliate or snub: *She is always putting her husband down.* **5** *(usually in passive)* to kill (an animal) painlessly when it is old or very ill: *The dog was getting deaf and blind so we had it put down. The poor cat was in pain and had to be put down.*

put forth *vt sep (old)* (of plants *etc*) to produce (leaves, shoots *etc*).

put forward *see* **bring forward**

put in *vt sep* **1** to insert or install: *We're having a new bath put in. The plumber put it in yesterday.* **2** to do (a certain amount of work *etc*): *He put in an hour's piano practice today.*

put in for *vt fus* to apply for, or claim: *Are you putting in for that job/grant?*

put off 1 *vt sep* to switch off (a light *etc*): *Please put the light off!* **2** *vt sep* to delay; to postpone: *He put off leaving/his departure till Thursday.* **3** *vt sep* to cancel an arranged meeting *etc* with (a person): *I had to put the Browns off because I had flu.* **4** *vt oblig sep* to cause (a person) to feel disgust or dislike: *The cheese looked nice but the smell put me off.*

put on *vt sep* **1** to switch on (a light *etc*): *Put the light on!* **2** to dress oneself in: *Which shoes are you going to put on!* **3** to add or increase: *The car put on speed. I've put on weight (* = become fatter). **4** to present or produce (a play *etc*): *They're putting on 'Hamlet' next week.* **5** to provide (*eg* transport): *They always put on extra buses between 8.00 and 9.00 a.m.* **6** to make a false show of; to feign: *She said she felt ill, but she was just putting it on. He put on a Spanish accent.*

put out *vt sep* **1** to extend (a hand *etc*): *He put out his hand to steady her.* **2** (of plants *etc*) to produce (shoots, leaves *etc*). **3** to extinguish (a fire, light *etc*): *The fire brigade soon put out the fire.* **4** to issue: *They put out a distress call.* **5** to cause bother or trouble to: *Don't put yourself out for my sake!* **6** to annoy: *I was put out by his decision.* **7** to strain or dislocate (a joint in the body): *He put his shoulder out trying to move the piano.*

put through *vt sep* **1** to arrange (a deal, agreement *etc*): *Has he managed to put that deal through?* **2** to connect by telephone: *Could you put me through to the manager? I'm trying to put you through. I want to put through a call to London.*

put together *vt oblig sep* to construct: *The vase broke, but*

put up

   I managed to put it together again (= mend it).
put up *vt sep* **1** to raise (a hand *etc*). **2** to build; to erect:
   They're putting up some new houses. **3** to fix (a notice
   etc) on a wall *etc*: *He put the poster up.* **4** to increase
   (a price *etc*): *They're putting up the fees again.* **5** to offer
   or show (resistance *etc*): *He's putting up a brave fight.*
   6 to provide (money) for a purpose: *He promised to put
   up the money for the scheme.* **7** to provide a bed *etc*
   for (a person) in one's home: *Can you put us up next
   Thursday night?*
put up with *vt fus* to bear patiently; to tolerate: *I cannot
   put up with all this noise.*
puzzle out *vt sep* to solve (a problem *etc*): *He managed to
   puzzle out the code.*
puzzle over/about *vt fus* to think long and carefully
   about, and try to solve (a problem *etc*): *I puzzled over
   the letter for hours.*

Q

quarrel with *vt fus (formal)* to disagree with (something):
   I wouldn't quarrel with your analysis of the situation.
queue up *vi (often with* for*)* to form, or stand in, a queue:
   *People are queuing up for tickets for the concert. They
   queued up to get into the theatre.*
quibble at/about *vt fus* to argue about or object to (something): *He quibbled at the price.*
quibble over *vt fus* to avoid discussing or agreeing to an
   important part of something by bringing up unimportant, trivial objections, arguments *etc*: *He agreed with
   the treaty in principle but quibbled over the details.*
quieten down *vi, vt sep* to make or become quiet: *I expect
   you to quieten down when I come into the classroom.
   That will quieten them down.*

R

rabbit on *vi (inf derog) (often with* **about***)* to talk at great length (about something): *What is he rabbiting on about?*

rake through *vt fus* to make a thorough search for something in (something): *I'm raking through these boxes of old clothes in case there is anything valuable in them.*

rake up *vt sep* to find out and tell or remind people about (something, usually unpleasant that would be better forgotten): *The newspaper reporters raked up a story about the politician stealing $20 from a shop when he was a boy.*

rally round *vi, vt fus* to come together for a joint action or effort, especially of support: *When John's business was in difficulty, his friends all rallied round (to help) him.*

ramble on *vi (derog) (usually with* **about***)* to talk for a long time in an aimless or confused way (about something): *The lecturer rambled on although the students were not listening.*

rap out *vt sep* to say quickly: *He rapped out his orders.*

rasp out *vt sep* to say (something) in a rasping voice: *The sergeant major rasped out an order to his troops.*

ration out *vt sep* to give or allow a ration of (food *etc*), *eg* to a number of people, over a period of time: *During the war meat had to be rationed out. She rationed out the sweets to the children.*

rattle off *vt sep (inf)* to say (something) quickly and usually without any feeling or expression: *The boy rattled off the poem as if he was reading a telephone directory.*

rattle on *vi (often with* **about***)* to talk quickly and at length (about something): *He rattled on all evening about his new job.*

rattle through *vt fus (inf)* to say or do (something) quickly: *The teacher rattled through his explanation so quickly that no-one could understand him.*

rave about/over *vt fus (inf)* to talk very enthusiastically (about something): *He's been raving about this new record he's heard.*

reach across/out/over *vt sep, vi (often with* **for***)* to try to touch, grasp or take (something) by stretching out one's hand: *He reached across/out/over for the last cake. He reached out (his hand) and took the last cake.*

read back *vt sep* to read (something) aloud to someone who has said it first: *The manager dictated the letter to his secretary, and then asked her to read it back to him.*

read in *vt sep* to look for or find (meanings, *eg* in a speech or letter which the speaker or writer did not intend): *You're reading rather a lot in. I'm sure he didn't mean that at all.*

read off *vt sep* to read (something) from a dial, instrument *etc*: *The engineer read off the temperatures one by one.*

read on *vi* to continue to read; to read further: *He paused for a few moments, and then read on.*

read out *vt sep* to read (something) aloud: *Read out the answers to the questions.*

read over/through *vt fus, vt sep* to read (something) from beginning to end: *I'll read over your manuscript, and let you know if I find any mistakes.*

read up *vt sep*, **read up on** *vt fus* to learn (something) by study: *I must read up on this. I must read this up before my exam.*

rear up *vi* **1** (especially of horses) to rear: *The horse reared up in fright.* **2** *(fig)* (of problems *etc*) to appear: *His stubbornness keeps on rearing up.*

reason with *vt fus* to argue with (a person) in order to persuade him to be more sensible: *We tried to reason with the worried mother but she went out alone in the storm to look for the child.*

rebound on/*(formal)* **upon** *vt fus* (of action *etc*) to have a usually bad or unfortunate effect on (the person performing the action *etc*): *The lies you tell sometimes rebound on you.*

reckon on/*(formal)* **upon** *vt fus* to depend on or expect (someone or something): *I was reckoning on meeting him tonight.*

reckon up *vt sep* to count or calculate (something): *When you reckon up the cost of eating in a restaurant it makes you decide to eat at home.*

reckon with *vt fus* to be prepared for (something); to expect (something); to expect (trouble, difficulties *etc*) from (a person *etc*): *I didn't reckon with all these problems. He's a man to be reckoned with.*

reckon without *vt fus* to expect not to have (something); to expect not to have (trouble, difficulties *etc*) from (someone); to make plans *etc* without taking (someone or something) into consideration: *I was reckoning without all the problems which keep coming up. He was reckoning without her mother's interference.*

reel in *vt sep* to pull (*eg* a fish out of the water) by winding the line to which it is attached on to a reel.

reel off *vt sep* to say or repeat (something) quickly and easily, without pausing: *He reeled off the list of names/ the parts of the verb 'to be'. He reeled it off without thinking.*

refrain from *vt fus (formal)* not to do (something): *You are asked to refrain from smoking.*

rely on/*(formal)* **upon** *vt fus* 1 to depend on or need (something or someone): *The people on the island relied on the supplies that were brought from the mainland.* 2 to trust (someone) to do something; to be certain that (something will happen): *We can't rely on him coming in time. He can't be relied on.*

rent out *vt sep* to allow (someone) to use a house, land *etc* which one owns, in exchange for money: *I own a cottage in the country which I rent out to tourists.*

report back *vi (sometimes with to)* to come again and report (to someone); to send a report (to someone): *Don't forget to report back here after you have finished* *these jobs. He was asked to study the matter in detail and report back to the committee.*

ride out *vt sep* **1** (of a ship) to keep afloat throughout (a storm *etc*): *to ride out a storm.* **2** *(fig)* to survive until (a period of difficulty) is past: *I think we'll ride out the crisis.*

ride up *vi* (of a skirt *etc*) to move gradually up out of its correct position: *I can't wear this skirt when I go to town, as it rides up when I walk.*

rig out *vt sep (inf)* to dress (oneself, someone else): *She was rigged out in rather odd clothes.*

rig up *vt sep* to build (something), usually quickly with whatever material is available: *They rigged up a rough shelter with branches and mud.*

ring back *vi, vt oblig sep* to telephone (someone who has telephoned): *If he is busy at the moment, he can ring me back. He'll ring back tomorrow.*

ring off *vi* to end a telephone call.

ring out *vi* to make a loud clear sound: *His voice rang out. A shot rang out.*

ring up 1 *vt sep* to record (the price of something sold) on a cash register: *You have rung up $5 and this book costs only $3.* **2** *vi, vt sep* to telephone someone: *He rang up to tell me the news. He rang me up too.*

rise above *vt fus (formal)* to ignore or not be affected by: *I know that you feel bad about having a stammer but you will just have to try and rise above it.*

roll in *vi (inf)* to come in or be got in large numbers or amounts: *They've started selling home-made cakes, and the money is just rolling in.*

roll on *vi* **1** (of a given time, day *etc*) (usually as a wish) to come soon: *Roll on the day when I can afford to buy a car.* **2** (of time) to pass or go by: *Time is rolling on and we haven't finished this job.*

roll up 1 *vt sep* to form (something) into a roll: *We'll need to roll up the carpet. He rolled up his sleeves* (= He rolled his sleeves up from the cuffs in order to leave his arms bare). **2** *vi (inf)* to arrive: *John rolled up half an* *hour late.* **3** *vi (usually in imperative)* (usually to a crowd, *eg* in a market, at a fair) to come near: *Roll up! Roll up! Come and see the bearded lady.*

root out/up *vt sep* **1** to pull up or tear out by the roots: *The gardener began to root out/up the weeds.* **2** *(fig)* to destroy completely: *We must do our best to root out disease and poverty.*

rope in *vt sep (inf)* to include (someone); to persuade (someone) to join in doing something: *We roped him in to help.*

rope off *vt sep* to put a rope around or across (a place) in order to prevent (other) people going in: *The end of the room was roped off for the most important guests.*

rough out *vt sep* to draw or explain (a rough sketch *etc* or idea): *I roughed out a diagram. He roughed out the plan to the others.*

round off 1 *vt sep* to make something smooth *etc*: *He rounded off the sharp corners with a file.* **2** *vi, vt sep (fig)* to complete successfully; to make a successful ending (to): *He rounded off his career by becoming president. He rounded the meal off with a glass of port. To round off, I shall perform my most famous trick.*

round on *vt fus (formal)* to attack (usually in words); to turn on: *He rounded on her, demanding to know where she had been.*

round up *vt sep* to collect together: *The farmer rounded up the sheep.*

rub along *vi (fig inf) (with* **with***)* to get on fairly well with (someone); to be fairly friendly with: *I rub along all right with my relations.*

rub down *vt sep* to clean or make smooth by rubbing: *Your horse needs rubbing down. Rub down the wall before you paint it.*

rub in *vt sep* **1** to make (a substance) go into the surface of something by rubbing: *She rubbed cream in to her hands. She rubbed it in firmly.* **2** *(inf)* to keep reminding someone of (something unpleasant): *I know I've lost my job — you don't have to keep rubbing it in!*

rub out *vt sep* to remove (a mark, writing *etc*) with a rubber; to erase: *He rubbed out what he had written and started again. He rubbed it out.*

rub up *vt sep* **1** to polish: *She rubbed up the silver until it shone.* **2** *(fig inf)* to refresh one's memory of; to remind oneself of: *I'm rubbing up my French before I go on holiday.*

rule out *vt sep* to leave out; not to consider: *We mustn't rule out the possibility of bad weather.*

run across *vt fus (inf)* to meet: *I ran across an old friend.*

run after *vt fus (inf)* to chase: *The dog ran after a cat.*

run aground *vi* (of a ship) to become stuck on rocks, the bottom of a shallow river *etc*: *The ship ran aground on a sandbank.*

run along *vi (inf)* to go away: *Run along now, children!*

run away *vi* **1** to escape: *He ran away from school. He ran away from prison.* **2** to steal: *He ran away with all her money.* **3** to go too fast *etc* to be controlled: *The horse ran away with him. (fig) Her enthusiasm ran away with her.*

run down **1** *vi* (of a clock, battery *etc*) to finish working: *My watch has run down — it needs rewinding.* **2** *vt sep* (of a vehicle or driver) to knock down: *He ran down a pedestrian.* **3** *vt sep (fig)* to speak badly of: *He is always running me down.*

run for *vt fus* to stand for election: *He is running for president.*

run in **1** *vi, vt sep* to get (a new engine *etc*) working properly: *The car is still running in. I only bought the car last month, so I am still running it in.* **2** *vt sep (sl)* to arrest: *The policeman ran him in for dangerous driving.*

run into **1** *vt fus (inf)* to meet: *I ran into her in the street.* **2** *vt fus, vt* to crash into or collide with: *The car ran into a lamp-post. I ran my bike into the back of a car.*

run off **1** *vt sep* to print: *He ran off 500 copies of the President's speech.* **2** *vi (with* **with***)* to steal or take away: *He ran off with all my money. (fig) He ran off with my wife.*

run out *vi* **1** (of a supply) to come to an end; to finish: *The food has run out.* **2** *(with of)* to have no more: *We've run out of money.* **3** *(inf: with on)* to leave or abandon someone: *His wife ran out on him.*

run over 1 *vt sep* (of a vehicle or driver) to knock down or drive over: *Don't let the dog out of the garden or it'll get run over.* **2** *vt fus* to repeat for practice: *Let's run over the plan again.*

run through *vt fus* to look at, deal with *etc*, one after another: *He ran through the names on the list. He ran through their instructions.*

run up *vt sep* **1** to hoist (a flag): *They ran up the school flag.* **2** *(inf)* to make quickly or roughly: *I can run up a dress in a couple of hours.* **3** to make (money) increase; to accumulate: *He ran up an enormous bill.*

rustle up *vt sep* *(sl)* to get or make quickly: *He rustled up some food and clean clothes.*

S

saddle up *vi, vt sep* to put a saddle on (a horse *etc*): *He saddled up and rode away. He saddled up the horses.*

sally forth *vi* **1** *(liter or very formal)* (of soldiers) to rush out (of a fort *etc*) in order to make an attack: *They sallied forth against the enemy.* **2** *(facet)* to go out (*eg* for a walk): *We sallied forth one morning to visit the museum.*

salt away *vt sep* *(inf)* to store up (money) for future use: *He has a pile of money salted away.*

save on *vt fus* to stop or prevent the wasting of (something, especially a form of fuel or power): *Cooking all the vegetables in one pot would save on gas. I think we should try to save on electricity/petrol.*

save up *vi, vt sep* to save: *He's been saving up for a new bike. He has been saving up all his fifty cent pieces for a new bike.*

savour of *vt fus (formal)* to have a suggestion or impression of (a usually bad quality, idea *etc*): *Their action savours of rebellion.*

saw off *vt sep* to cut (a piece) from something by sawing: *He had sawn the branch off.*

saw up *vt sep* to saw (wood *etc*) into pieces: *He sawed the tree up for firewood.*

scale down, up *vt sep* to decrease or increase (*eg* wages) by a certain scale: *The wages for workers of all grades will be scaled up by five per cent.*

scare away/off *vt sep* to make (someone or something) go away or stay away because of fear: *The birds were scared away by the dog. We keep a cat to scare the mice off.*

scoop out *vt sep* to get or dig out with a scooping movement: *She scooped some ice-cream out on to his plate. He scooped out a hole in the sand with his hands.*

scoop up *vt sep* to pick up with a scoop or with a scooping movement: *She scooped up the pebbles in her hands.*

score off *vt fus* to make (a person) appear foolish, especially in conversation: *He's always scoring off his wife in public.*

scrape along *vi* to manage to live in spite of difficulties: *We don't have much money but we scrape along somehow.*

scrape through *vi, vt fus* to only just avoid failing (an examination *etc*): *He scraped through his exams. He took the test and just scraped through.*

scrape together/up *vt sep* to manage (with difficulty) to find (enough money, people *etc* to do something): *His parents scraped up enough (money) to buy him a bicycle. I'll try to scrape a team together for the game.*

scratch about *vi* (of birds *etc*) to scratch (the ground *etc*) looking for food *etc*: *The birds were scratching about (for food) in the snow.*

scratch out *vt sep* to delete (a word *etc*) by drawing a line or lines untidily through it: *A name was written in the book, but it had been scratched out.*

screen off *vt sep* to separate or hide (something) with, or as if with, a screen: *Part of the room was screened off. The vegetable garden was screened off by a row of bushes.*

screw up *vt sep* **1** to fasten with screws: *The windows are screwed up so that they won't open.* **2** to twist or wrinkle (the face or features): *The baby screwed up its face and began to cry. She screwed her nose up in disgust.* **3** to crumple (a piece of paper *etc*) into a ball: *She screwed up the letter.*

scrub down *vt sep* to clean by scrubbing thoroughly: *He scrubbed himself down after clearing the rubbish out of the attic.*

scrub out *vt sep* to clean the inside of (*eg* a bowl) by scrubbing: *Please scrub the bath out!*

seal in *vt sep* to enclose (something) within a container *etc* so that it cannot escape: *The full flavour of the coffee will remain sealed in until the tin is opened.*

seal off *vt sep* to prevent all approach to, or exit from, (an area): *The police have sealed off the area where the murdered girl was found.*

see about *vt fus* to attend to or deal with (a matter): *I'll see about this tomorrow. Will you see about putting the children to bed?*

see off *vt usually sep* **1** to accompany (a person starting on a journey) to the airport, railway station *etc* from which he is to leave: *He saw me off at the station.* **2** (*inf*) to chase away: *There were some children stealing my apples but my dog soon saw them off.*

see out 1 *vt oblig sep* to lead or accompany (a person) to the door or exit of a building *etc*: *The maid will see you out.* **2** *vt sep* (*inf*) to last longer than: *These old trees will see us all out.*

see over *vt fus* to visit and inspect (*eg* a house that is for sale): *We'll see over the house on Friday.*

see through 1 *vt oblig sep* to give support to (a person, plan *etc*) until the end is reached: *She had a lot of difficulties, but his family saw her through. Will this*

money *see* you *through* till the end of the week? I'd like
to *see* the job *through*. **2** *vt fus* not to be deceived by
(a person, trick *etc*): We soon *saw through* him and his
little plan.

see to *vt fus* to attend to, to deal with (someone or something): I must *see to* the baby. I can't come now — I've
got this job to *see to*.

seek out *vt sep* (*formal or liter*) to find by searching: He
sought out all his old friends. There's enough trouble in
the world without *seeking* it *out*.

seize on/(*formal*) **upon** *vt fus* to accept (an idea, suggestion *etc*) with enthusiasm: I suggested a cycling holiday,
and he *seized on* the idea.

seize up *vi* (of machinery *etc*) to get stuck and stop working: The car *seized up* yesterday.

sell off *vt sep* to sell (goods) quickly and cheaply: They're
selling off their old stock.

sell out 1 *vi, vt sep* (*sometimes with* of) to sell all of one's
stock or supply of something: We have *sold out of*
children's socks. We *sold out* our entire stock. We had a
stock of those plates, but we've *sold out*. **2** *vi* to be all
sold: The second-hand records *sold out* within minutes
of the sale starting. **3** *vi, vt sep* (*usually with* to) to join
or assist (an enemy): The newspaper published evidence
that an important politician had *sold out* to the enemy.
4 *vi, vt sep* (*sometimes with* to) to sell one's share
in a business: I got tired of filling in complicated tax-
forms, so I *sold out* and went to live in the country.

sell up *vi, vt sep* to sell a house, business *etc*: He has *sold
up* his share of the business. I'm thinking of *selling up*
and retiring.

send away for *vt fus* to order (goods) by post: I've *sent
away for* some things that I saw in the catalogue.

send down *vt sep* to expel (a student) from a university.

send for *vt fus* to ask (somebody) to come, or order
(goods) to be delivered: She was very ill, and her son
was *sent for*. I've *sent for* some meat from the butcher's.
You'll have to *send for* a plumber to mend that pipe. I'll

send for a taxi.

send in *vt sep* to offer or submit (something *eg* for a competition): *Let's send in our names for the essay competition. Suggestions for the next meeting must be sent in by Friday.*

send off *vt sep* **1** to dispatch (by post): *Have you sent off that letter yet?* **2** to accompany (a person) to the place, or be at the place, where he will start a journey: *A great crowd gathered at the station to send the football team off.*

send off for *vt fus* to send away for: *I must send off for that dress I saw advertised in the Sunday newspaper.*

send on *vt sep* **1** to re-address (a letter *etc*) and post it to a person who is not at his usual address: *Do you want your mail sent on while you're on holiday?* **2** to send (*eg* a person, luggage *etc*) ahead, or in advance: *She sent them on to find a hotel while she waited with the luggage. She didn't want to carry her heavy cases, so she sent them on ahead of her.*

send out *vt sep* **1** to distribute *eg* by post: *A notice has been sent out to all employees. They've already sent out the invitations to the wedding.* **2** (of plants *etc*) to produce: *This plant has sent out some new shoots.*

send up *vt sep* (*inf*) to ridicule (someone or something), especially through satire or parody: *In his latest play, he sends up university teachers. Don't send him up — he's easily embarrassed.*

separate off *vt sep* to make or keep (a part or parts) separate: *Part of the office is separated off for the use of the manager. His room is separated off from the rest of the office.*

separate out *vt sep* to make or keep (things) separate or distinct: *You're confusing two ideas — you should try to separate them out in your mind. Try to separate out all the good apples and/from all the bad ones.*

separate up *vt sep* (*often with* **into**) to divide: *The house has been separated up into different flats.*

serve out *vt sep* to distribute or give (a portion of food *etc*) to each of a number of people: *She served out the pudding. You haven't served the ice-cream out fairly!*

serve up *vi, vt sep* to start serving (a meal): *Is it time to serve up (the meal)?*

set about *vt fus* **1** to begin: *She set about planning her holiday. How will you set about this task?* **2** (*formal*) to attack: *When I refused to give him money, he set about me with a stick.*

set apart *vt sep* (*formal: usually with* **from**) **1** to place separately: *Their house was set apart from the others in the street.* **2** to cause (a person or thing) to be or seem different: *His academic brilliance set him apart from the other children.*

set aside *vt sep* **1** to keep (something) for a special use or purpose: *He set aside some cash for use at the weekend.* **2** (*formal*) to reject: *I warned them not to do it, but my objections were set aside.*

set back *vt usually sep* **1** to delay the progress of: *His illness set him back a bit at school.* **2** (*inf*) to cause (a person) a lot of expense: *The new carpet must have set you back a few hundred dollars.* **3** (*sometimes with* **from**) to put (something) at a slight distance from something: *The house was set back from the road and partly hidden by trees.*

set down *vt sep* **1** (of a bus *etc*) to stop and let (passengers) out: *The bus set us down outside the post-office.* **2** to write: *He tried to write his essay, but found it difficult to set his thoughts down.*

set forth (*old: formal or liter*) **1** *vi* to start a journey: *What time did he set forth?* **2** *vt sep* to exhibit or explain: *The goods were set forth for display. His opinions are clearly set forth in this document.*

set in *vi* (of weather, seasons, feelings *etc*) to begin or become established: *Winter has set in early. Boredom soon set in among the children.*

set off 1 *vi* (*sometimes with* **on**) to start a journey: *We set off to go to the beach. We set off on our journey.* **2** *vt usually sep* to cause (someone or something) to start doing something: *She had almost stopped crying, but his harsh words set her off again.* **3** *vt sep* to make (something) more beautiful; to look well with (something): *The frame sets off the picture well.* **4** *vt sep* to explode (bombs *etc*) or ignite (fireworks *etc*): *You should let your father set off all the fireworks.*

set on *see* **set upon**

set out 1 *vi* to start a journey: *He set out to explore the countryside. When are we setting out on our trip?* **2** *vi* to intend: *I didn't set out to prove him wrong.* **3** *vt sep* to exhibit, display or explain: *The goods are set out in the shop window. He always sets his ideas out very clearly.*

set to *vi* to start to do something (vigorously): *They set to, and finished the work the same day.*

set up 1 *vt sep* to establish: *When was the organization set up? A committee of inquiry has been set up.* **2** *vi, vt usually sep* to (help a person to) start working in a business *etc*: *He set (himself) up as a bookseller. His father set him up in business.* **3** *vt sep* to arrange or construct: *He set up the apparatus for the experiment. The type for the book is being set up.* **4** *vt oblig sep (slightly inf)* to improve the health or spirits of (a person): *The holiday has really set us up again.*

set upon *vt fus (also* **set on***: usually in passive: formal)* to attack: *He set upon me in the dark. He was set upon by thieves.*

settle down 1 *vi, vt sep* to (cause to) become quiet, calm and peaceful: *He waited for the audience to settle down before he spoke. Settle down, children! She settled the baby down at last.* **2** *vi, vt refl sep* to make oneself comfortable: *She settled (herself) down in the back of the car and went to sleep.* **3** *vi* to begin to concentrate on something, *eg* work: *He settled down to (do) his schoolwork.* **4** *vi* to (begin to) work, live *etc* in a quiet, calm *etc* way: *He is settling down well in his new school/job. Isn't it time you got married and settled down?*

settle for *vt fus* to accept (something that is not completely satisfactory): *We wanted two single rooms at the hotel, but had to settle for a room with two beds instead.*

settle in *vi* to arrange possessions *etc* satisfactorily after moving into a new house; to become used to one's new surroundings when starting a new job *etc*: *We move house on Friday, but we'll take another week to settle in.*

settle on / *(formal)* **upon** *vt fus* to agree about or decide (something): *They at last settled on a plan after much arguing.*

settle up *vi* to pay a bill: *He asked the waiter for the bill, and settled up.*

settle up with *vt fus* to pay money owed to (somebody): *We shall have to settle up with the travel agent tomorrow.*

settle with *vt fus* **1** to do something unpleasant to (someone who has done wrong to one): *He has told everyone I'm a liar and a cheat — I'll settle with him later!* **2** to settle up with.

sew up *vt sep* to fasten completely or mend by sewing: *I've cut out the dress, but I haven't sewn it up yet. I must sew up this hole in my skirt. The surgeon sewed up the wound.*

shack up together *vi (sl)* (of eg a man and woman not married to each other) to live together: *They couldn't afford a wedding so they just shacked up together.*

shack up with *vt fus (sl)* to live with (someone one is not married to): *He has been shacking up with his secretary for years.*

shade in *vt sep* to mark the dark parts of (a picture *etc*): *I've done the outline of the drawing, but I haven't yet shaded it in.*

shake off *vt sep* to rid oneself of (something unwanted): *By running very hard he managed to shake off his pursuers. He soon shook off the illness.*

shake out *vt sep* to cause to spread or unfold by shaking:

She shook out the dress and hung it up after she removed it from the suitcase.

shake up *vt sep (inf)* to disturb or rouse (people) so as to make them more energetic: *The new headmistress will shake the school up.*

share out *vt sep* to divide (something) between several people *etc*: *She shared the pudding out.*

sheer off/away *vi* to turn aside or swerve: *The speed-boat seemed to be heading straight towards some swimmers but sheered off at the last moment.*

shell out *vi, vt sep (inf derog)* to pay out (money): *I was the one who had to shell out for the food. I had to shell out fifty dollars. I refuse to shell out any more money on a project that's bound to fail.*

ship off *vt sep (inf: often derog)* to send away: *The children have been shipped off to boarding-school.*

shoot down *vt sep (often fig)* to hit (*eg* a plane) with *eg* a shell and cause it to crash into the ground: *They shot down six of the enemy's planes. He was shot down in flames* (= severely criticized) *when he suggested accepting the offer.*

shoot up *vi* to grow or increase rapidly: *Prices have shot up. After last week's rain, the weeds have shot up.*

shop around *vi* to compare prices, quality of goods *etc* at several shops before buying anything: *This isn't exactly what I want, so I think I'll shop around a bit before I make any decision.*

shore up *vt sep* to support with props *etc*; to prop up: *The fire damaged the building so badly that it had to be shored up. (fig) The government shored up the business with extra money.*

shout down *vt sep* to make it impossible for a speaker to be heard (*eg* at a meeting) by shouting, jeering *etc* very loudly: *The meeting had to be abandoned because certain people in the audience were determined to shout down all the speakers.*

shout out *vi, vt sep* to shout (something): *The teacher scolded the child for shouting out (the answers) in class.*

shove off *vi (inf: especially in the imperative: sometimes offensive)* to go away: *Shove off and leave me alone! Will you please just shove off! I think I'll shove off now.*

show off 1 *vt sep* to show or display for admiration: *He showed off his new car by taking it to work. She is just showing off her knowledge of French.* **2** *vi (inf derog)* to try to impress others with one's possessions, ability to do something *etc*: *She is just showing off — she wants everyone to know how well she speaks French.*

show up 1 *vt sep* to make (faults *etc*) obvious: *This kind of light really shows up the places where I've mended this coat.* **2** *vt sep (inf)* to reveal the faults, mistakes *etc* of (a person): *Ann was so neat that she really showed me up.* **3** *vi* to stand out clearly: *The scratches showed up badly on the photograph.* **4** *vi (inf)* to appear or arrive: *I waited for hours, but she never showed up.*

shrivel up *vi, vt sep* to shrivel: *The flowers shrivelled up. The heat shrivelled up the flowers.*

shrug off *vt sep* to dismiss, get rid of or treat as unimportant: *She shrugged off all criticism and calmly went on with the project.*

shut down *vi, vt sep* (of a factory *etc*) to close or be closed, for a time or permanently: *There is a rumour going round that the factory is going to (be) shut down.*

shut off *vt sep* **1** to stop (an engine working, a liquid flowing *etc*): *Is there any way of shutting off that part of the motor? I'll need to shut the gas off before I repair the fire.* **2** *(usually refl)* to keep away (from); to make separate (from): *He shut himself off from the rest of the world.*

shut up 1 *vi, vt sep (inf)* to (cause to) stop speaking: *Tell them to shut up! That'll shut him up!* **2** *vt sep* to close and lock: *It's time to shut up the shop.* **3** *vt sep* to shut in: *He shut himself up in his room.*

side with *vt fus (often with* **against***)* to give support to (a person, group *etc*) in an argument *etc*: *Don't side with him against us!*

sigh for *vt fus (liter)* to regret: *He sighed for his lost* *opportunities.*

sign away *vt sep* to give away or transfer, by signing one's name: *She signed away her money to her daughter.*

sign in, out *vi* to record one's arrival (especially at work) or departure by writing one's name: *We have to sign in when we arrive at the office. He signed in at the hotel when he arrived.*

sign off *(inf)* 1 *vi* to stop work: *Because of the bad weather, we signed off at four o'clock.* 2 *vi* (of a radio channel *etc*) to stop broadcasting: *Radio 3 signed off at midnight.* 3 *vt sep* to sign a certificate of (someone's) unfitness to work: *The doctor has signed me off for a month.*

sign on *vi, vt sep* to engage (oneself) for work *etc*: *He signed on a new crew in London. Every week more people sign on at the Labour Exchange.*

sign up 1 *vi* to join an organization or make an agreement to do something *etc* by writing one's name: *I have signed up for a place on the outing next week.* 2 *vt sep* to engage for work by making a legal contract: *The football club have signed up two new players for this season.*

silt up *vi, vt sep* to (cause to) become blocked by mud *etc*: *The harbour had gradually silted up, so that large boats could no longer use it. Mud from the river silted up the harbour.*

simmer down *vi (inf: usually in imperative)* to calm down: *Do simmer down — there's no point in being angry. She'll soon simmer down.*

sing out *vi (inf)* to shout or call out: *Sing out when you're ready to go.*

single out *vt sep* to choose or pick out for special treatment: *He was singled out to receive special thanks for his help.*

sink in *vi* 1 to be fully understood: *The news took a long time to sink in.* 2 to be absorbed: *The surface water on the paths will soon sink in.*

siphon off *vt sep (inf derog)* to take (part of something) away gradually and illegally: *He siphoned off some of the club's funds for his own use.*

sit back *vi* to rest and take no part in an activity: *He just sat back and let it all happen.*

sit down *vi, vt sep* to (cause to) take a seat or take a sitting position: *Let's sit down over here. He sat the child down on the floor.*

sit in *vi* **1** (*with* **on**) to be present at (a meeting *etc*) without being an actual member: *The inspector sat in on the trainee teacher's lesson.* **2** to hold a sit-in: *The students seem tired of sitting in.*

sit out *vi, vt sep* **1** to remain seated during a dance: *Let's sit (this one) out.* **2** to remain inactive and wait until the end of: *They'll try to sit out the crisis. We'll sit out to the very end.*

sit up 1 *vi, vt sep* to (cause to) rise to a sitting position: *Can the patient sit up? The nurse sat the patient up against his pillows.* **2** *vi* to sit with one's back straight: *Do sit up in your chair and stop slouching!* **3** *vi* to remain awake, not going to bed: *I sat up until 3 a.m. waiting for you!* **4** *vi* (*fig inf*) to pay attention: *That'll make them all sit up!*

size up *vt sep* (*slightly inf*) to form an opinion about the worth, nature *etc* of (a person, situation *etc*): *I'm not very good at sizing people up quickly. He sized up the situation and acted immediately.*

skate over *vt fus* (*inf*) to pass over (a subject, difficulty *etc*) quickly, trying to avoid taking it into consideration: *He always skates over the problems attached to his plans.*

slacken off *vi, vt sep* to become or make slack or slacken: *Slacken off that rope a bit! The rope slackened off.*

slap down *vt sep* (*inf*) to dismiss or dispose of (opposition *etc*) abruptly: *My suggestion was immediately slapped down.*

sleep around *vi* (*inf often derog*) to be in the habit of having sexual intercourse with a number of different people; to be promiscuous: *She finally got married and* *stopped sleeping around.*

sleep in *vi* **1** to sleep at one's place of work: *She employs a gardener who lives in the village, but the maid is required to sleep in.* **2** *(inf)* to sleep late in the morning; to oversleep: *I slept in by mistake and was very late for work.*

sleep off *vt sep* to recover from (something) by sleeping: *She's in bed sleeping off the effects of the party. I have a slight infection, but I think I'll manage to sleep it off.*

sleep on *vt fus (inf)* to put off making a decision about (something) overnight: *I'll sleep on it and let you know tomorrow.*

sleep out *vi* to sleep away from one's place of work: *She has a housekeeper who sleeps out.*

sleep together *vi (euph)* (of two people) to have, or be in the habit of having, sexual intercourse: *Do you think John and Jane are sleeping together?*

sleep with *vt fus (euph)* to have, or be in the habit of having, sexual intercourse with: *Many unmarried girls sleep with their boyfriends nowadays. His wife has a lot of male friends but I don't think she ever sleeps with any of them.*

slick down *vt sep (inf)* to make (hair *etc*) smooth: *His hair was slicked down with hair-cream.*

slip into *vt fus* to put on (clothes) quickly: *She slipped into her nightdress.*

slip off **1** *vt sep* to take (clothes) off quickly: *Slip off your shoes.* **2** *vi* to move away noiselessly or hurriedly: *We'll slip off when no-one's looking.*

slip on *vt sep* to put on (clothes) quickly: *She got out of bed and slipped on her dressing-gown.*

slip up *vi* to make a mistake; to fail to do something: *They certainly slipped up badly over the new appointment.*

slop about/around *vi (inf)* **1** to move about (in), or play (with, anything wet or sloppy): *The children were slopping about in the puddles.* **2** *(with* **in***)* to go about dressed in an untidy way: *I like to slop around in old clothes at the weekend.*

slope off *vi (sl)* to go away, especially secretively and without warning: *When I next looked round for him, he had taken his chance and sloped off.*

slow down/up *vi, vt sep* to make or become slower: *The police were warning drivers to slow down because of the fog. The snow was slowing up the traffic.*

smell out *vt sep* **1** to find (as if) by smelling: *We buried the dog's bone, but he smelt it out again.* **2** to fill (a place) with a very strong, unpleasant smell: *That cheese is smelling the room out.*

smile on *vt fus (liter)* to be favourable to: *Fate smiled on us.*

smoke out *vt sep* to drive (an animal *etc*) into the open by filling its burrow, hiding-place *etc* with smoke: *They decided to smoke the fox out.*

smooth away *vt sep (often fig)* to cause to disappear by smoothing: *I think we'll be able to smooth away these little difficulties. You can't smooth away wrinkles on your face.*

smooth over *vt sep* to make (problems *etc*) less important: *It's no good trying to smooth over the quarrel — they've been enemies for years.*

snap up *vt sep* to grab eagerly: *I saw this bargain in the shop and snapped it up straight away.*

snarl up *vt sep (inf)* to cause to become confused, tangled *etc* and stop working, moving *etc* smoothly: *A loose screw had fallen into the machinery and snarled it up.*

sniff out *vt sep (fig inf)* to discover or detect (by using the sense of smell): *I'll see if I can sniff out the cause of the trouble.*

snipe at *vt fus* to shoot at (someone) from a hidden position: *The rebels had occupied a block of flats and were sniping at the government troops from the windows. (fig) As a politician he is quite used to being sniped at in the newspapers.*

snuff out *vt sep* **1** to extinguish the flame of (a candle *etc*): *He snuffed out the candle by squeezing the wick between his thumb and fore-finger.* **2** to cause to come to a sudden end: *Opposition was quickly snuffed out.*

soak off *vt sep* to remove by soaking: *A good way to get a stamp off an envelope is to soak it off.*

soak out *vi, vt sep* to (cause *eg* dirt to) disappear by soaking: *I've got a dirty mark on my dress, but I may be able to soak it out. The dirt will soak out in water.*

soak up *vt sep* to draw in or suck up; to absorb: *He used a large piece of blotting-paper to soak up the ink. You'd better soak that spilt coffee up with a cloth before it stains the carpet. (fig) That child absolutely soaks up information!*

sober up *vi, vt sep (inf)* to make or become (more) sober: *You'll have to sober up if you want to be able to drive home. Black coffee will sober him up.*

soften up 1 *vi, vt sep* to (cause to) become soft: *The wax will soften up if you heat it. Heat will soften it up.* **2** *vt sep (usually inf fig)* to weaken or make less able to resist something which follows: *He sent his aunt a bunch of flowers to soften her up before asking for a loan.*

sort out *vt sep* **1** to separate (one lot or type of) things from a general mixture: *I'll try to sort out some books that he might like.* **2** to correct, improve, solve *etc*: *You must sort out your business affairs before you are forced to close down.* **3** *(sl)* to attend to, usually by punishing or reprimanding: *I'll soon sort you out, you evil little man!*

sound off *vi (derog sl)* to speak loudly and freely, especially while complaining: *She was sounding off about the price of tea.*

sound out *vt sep* to try to find out (someone's thoughts and plans *etc*): *Will you sound out your father on this? I sounded out his views in my letter.*

soup up *vt sep (sl)* to tune (an engine) so as to make it go faster than normal: *The mechanic souped up his car before he set out for the race.*

speak for *vt fus* to give an opinion *etc* on behalf of (someone else): *I myself don't have any objections to your suggestions, but I can't speak for Liz and Frank.*

speak out *vi* to say boldly what one thinks: *I don't like to make a fuss, but I feel the time has come to speak out.*

speak up *vi* to speak (more) loudly: *Speak up! We can't hear you!*

speed up 1 *vi* to increase speed: *The car speeded up as it left the town.* **2** *vt sep* to quicken the rate of: *We are trying to speed up production.*

spell out *vt sep* **1** to say the letters of (a word) in order: *Could you spell that word out for me?* **2** to give a highly detailed explanation of (something): *He's a bit stupid — you'll have to spell it out for him.*

spin out *vt sep* to cause to last a (usually unnecessarily) long or longer time: *He spun out his speech for an extra five minutes.*

spirit away *vt sep* to carry away or remove secretly and suddenly, as if by magic: *The actress left the hotel by a back door and was spirited away before the reporters discovered the plan.*

spread out 1 *vi, vt sep* to extend or stretch out: *The fields spread out in front of him. He spread out the rug on the grass.* **2** *vt sep* to distribute over a wide area or period of time: *She spread the leaflets out on the table. She spread out her trips to town over six weeks.* **3** *vi* to scatter and go in different directions, in order to cover a wider area: *They spread out when they entered the field and began to search the ground.*

spring back *vi* to return suddenly to a former, usually normal, shape or position: *When using a bow and arrow, you should wear a wristguard to protect your wrist when the bowstring springs back.*

spring up *vi* to develop or appear suddenly: *Weeds seemed to have sprung up all over the garden.* (fig) *New buildings are springing up everywhere.*

sprout up *vi* (of plants or *inf* of children) to grow: *That fruit bush has sprouted up fast. At the age of fourteen he really began to sprout up.*

spruce up *vi, vt sep (inf)* to make (oneself or somebody else) smarter: *I'll go and spruce up before going out. She brushed his jacket and spruced him up. Spruce yourself up a bit!*

spur on *vt sep* to urge (a horse) to go faster, using spurs, or (a person) to make greater efforts: *He spurred his horse on. The thought of the prize spurred her on.*

spy on/*(formal)* **upon** *vt fus* to watch (a person *etc*) secretly: *The police had been spying on the gang for several months. (inf) Our next-door neighbours are always spying on us.*

square up (with) *vi, vt fus (inf)* to settle (an account): *I'll pay for the meal and we can square up/you can square up with me afterwards.*

squeeze up *vi* to move closer together: *Could you all squeeze up on the bench and make room for me to sit down?*

stab at *vt fus* to make poking or stabbing movements in the direction of: *The soldiers kept stabbing at them with their bayonets.*

stake out *vt sep* to mark the boundary of (a piece of territory *etc*) with stakes: *They are staking out the ground for a new football pitch.*

stammer out *vt sep* to say (something) with a stammer; to stammer (something): *He stammered his explanation out with difficulty. He stammered out an explanation.*

stamp out *vt sep* 1 to put out or extinguish (a fire) by stamping on it: *She stamped the remains of the fire out. The fire has been stamped out.* 2 to crush or subdue (a rebellion *etc*): *The new king stamped out all opposition to his rule.*

stand aside *vi* to move to one side or withdraw out of someone's way: *He stood aside to let me past.*

stand back *vi* to move backwards or away; not to stand too close: *A crowd gathered round the injured man, but a policeman ordered everyone to stand back.*

stand by 1 *vi* to watch (something happening) without doing anything: *I couldn't just stand by while he was* *hitting the child.* **2** *vi* to be ready to act: *The police are standing by in case of trouble.* **3** *vt fus* to support or maintain: *She stood by him throughout his trial. I stand by my principles.*

stand down *vi* to withdraw *eg* from a contest: *Two of the candidates have stood down.*

stand for *vt fus* **1** to be a candidate for election to (*eg* Parliament): *He stood for Parliament/one of the constituencies.* **2** to be an abbreviation for: *HQ stands for Headquarters.* **3** to represent: *I hate commercialism and all it stands for.* **4** to tolerate: *I won't stand for her rudeness.*

stand in *vi* (usually with **for**) to take another person's place, job *etc* for a time: *Could you stand in for me as chairman of the meeting? The leading actor was ill and another actor stood in for him.*

stand out *vi* **1** to be noticeable because exceptional: *They were all pretty, but she stood out among them.* **2** (*formal*) to go on resisting or to refuse to yield: *The garrison stood out (against the besieging army) as long as possible.*

stand over *vt fus* to supervise (a person) closely: *I have to stand over him to make him do his schoolwork.*

stand to *vi* (especially military) to prepare for action: *The troops were ordered to stand to in case of attack.*

stand up *vt sep* (*sl*) not to keep a promise to meet (*eg* a girl-friend): *You've stood me up three times this week!*

stand up for *vt fus* to support or defend (*eg* a person) in a dispute *etc*: *I thanked him for standing up for me/my proposals.*

stand up to *vt fus* to show resistence to: *He stood up to the bigger boys who tried to bully him. These chairs have stood up to very hard wear.*

stare out *vt sep* to stare at (a person, animal *etc*) for longer than he/it can stare at oneself: *People used to be taught that a wolf would not attack them if they stared it out.*

start back *vi* **1** to begin a return journey: *We ought to start back soon.* **2** to jump or step backwards suddenly (*eg* in fright): *He started back in terror when he saw the snake.*

start off 1 *vi* to begin a journey: *It's time we started off.* **2** *vt sep* to cause or allow (something) to begin, (someone) to start doing something *etc*: *The money lent to him by his father started him off as a bookseller. She had stopped crying, but his remark started her off again.*

start out *vi* to begin a journey; to start off: *To arrive there in the afternoon we shall have to start out at dawn.*

start up *vi, vt sep* to (cause to) begin or begin working *etc*: *The machine suddenly started up. Her eye trouble has started up again. What started it up again? He has started up a new boys' club in the town.*

starve out *vt sep* (of a besieging army *etc*) to force (a city, garrison *etc*) to surrender, by preventing supplies of food from reaching it.

stay behind *vi* to remain in a place after others have left it: *They all left the office at five o'clock, but he stayed behind to finish some work/to wait for me.*

stay in *vi* to remain in one's house *etc* and not go out of doors: *I'm staying in tonight to watch television.*

stay out *vi* to remain out of doors and not return to one's house *etc*: *The children mustn't stay out after 9 p.m.*

stay up *vi* not to go to bed: *The children wanted to stay up and watch television. Don't stay up for me* (= keep awake until I return), *as I shall be home late.*

steam off *vt sep* to remove (*eg* a stamp from an envelope): *She held the letter over the kettle to steam off the stamp.*

steam up *vi, vt sep* to (cause to) become covered with condensation: *Kitchen windows steam up/become steamed up easily.*

step aside *vi* to move to one side: *He stepped aside to let me pass. (fig) He's getting too old for the job, and should step aside for a younger man.*

step in *vi* to intervene: *The children began to quarrel, and I thought it was time I stepped in.*

step out *vi* to walk with a long(er) and (more) energetic stride: *Once he reached the mountain ridge, he was able* to *step out.*

step up *vt sep* to increase: *The firm must step up production this year.*

stick around *vi (sl)* to remain (in a place), usually in the hope of some future advantage *etc*: *If you stick around, we might have a job for you in a week or two.*

stick at *vt fus* 1 to hesitate, or refuse, *eg* to do (especially something wrong): *He probably wouldn't stick at murder to get what he wants.* 2 to persevere with (work *etc*): *He must learn to stick at his job.*

stick by *vt fus* to support or be loyal to (a person): *His friends stuck by him when he was in trouble.*

stick on *vt sep* to stick (an adhesive label, stamp *etc*) on something: *He locked his case and stuck a label on.*

stick out 1 *vi, vt sep* to (cause to) project: *He stuck his foot out and tripped her. His front teeth stick out.* 2 *vi* to be noticeable: *She has red hair that always sticks out in a crowd.*

stick out for *vt fus (inf)* to refuse to accept less than: *The men are sticking out for a fifteen per cent pay rise.*

stick to/with *vt fus* not to abandon: *We've decided to stick to our previous plan. If you stick to (= remain loyal to) me, I'll stick to you. He stuck with (= remained in) the firm for twenty years.*

stick together 1 *vi, vt sep* to (cause to) be fastened together with glue *etc*: *These stamps are sticking together.* 2 *vi* (of friends *etc*) to remain loyal to each other: *They've stuck together all these years.*

stick up for *vt fus* to speak in defence of (a person *etc*): *When my father is angry with me, my mother always sticks up for me.*

stink out *vt sep (inf)* to fill (a place) with a stink: *The fish has stunk the whole house out.*

stir up *vt sep* to cause (trouble *etc*): *He was trying to stir up trouble at the factory.*

stitch up *vt sep* to close by stitching: *Could you stitch up the hole in my skirt? The doctor stitched up the wound.*

stock up *vi*, *vt sep (often with* **on** *or* **with**) to accumulate a supply of (something): *The boys were stocking up on chocolate and lemonade for their walk. There is likely to be a shortage of sugar, so we had better stock up (our supplies).*

stoke up 1 *vi*, *vt sep* to stoke: *Have they stoked up (the fires)?* **2** *vi (inf: sometimes with* **with**) to eat plenty: *You ought to stoke up (with food) before going up the mountain.*

stop in *vi (inf)* to remain at home: *I'll stop in tonight.*

stop off *vi (inf)* to make a halt on a journey *etc*: *We stopped off at Edinburgh to see the castle.*

stop out *vi (inf)* not to return home: *He stopped out all night.*

stop over *vi (inf)* to make a stay of a night or more: *We're planning to stop over in Amsterdam.*

stop up *vt sep* to block: *My nose is stopped up. Some rubbish got into the drain and stopped it up.*

store up *vt sep* to collect and keep (for future need): *I don't know why she stores up all those old magazines. (fig) She stored up the joke to tell her husband later.*

stow away 1 *vi* to hide oneself (on a ship, aircraft *etc*) before its departure, in order to travel on it without paying the fare: *He stowed away on a cargo ship for New York.* **2** *vt sep* to put or pack in a (secret) place until required: *My jewellery has been safely stowed away in the bank.*

straighten out/up 1 *vi*, *vt sep* to make or become straight: *Their house is just where the lane straightens out. He was bending over his work, but straightened up when he saw me.* **2** *vt sep* to tidy: *She straightened the room up.* **3** *vt sep* to remove confusion *etc* in: *He's trying to straighten out the facts.*

strain off *vt sep* to remove (liquid) from *eg* vegetables by using a sieve *etc*: *When the potatoes were cooked, she strained off the water.*

strap in *vt sep* to confine with a strap, *eg* by fastening a safety-belt in a car: *I won't start this car till you've strapped yourself in. Have you strapped the child in?*

strap up *vt sep* to fasten or bind with a strap, or other form of binding: *His injured knee was washed and neatly strapped up* (= bandaged). *He has broken a rib and the doctor has strapped it up.*

stretch out *vi, vt sep* in moving the body, to straighten or extend: *She stretched out a hand for the child to hold. He stretched (himself) out on the grass. She stretched out on the bed.*

strike at *vt fus* to attempt to strike, or aim a blow at (a person *etc*): *He struck at the dog with his stick.*

strike down *vt sep* (*formal: usually fig*) to hit or knock (a person) so that he falls down: *He was struck down by* (= was killed by or afflicted with) *a terrible disease.*

strike off *vt sep* to remove or erase (*eg* a doctor's name) from a professional register *etc* for misconduct: *He/His name was struck off.*

strike out 1 *vt sep* to erase or cross out (a word *etc*): *He read the essay and struck out a word here and there.* **2** *vi* to start fighting, attempt to hit someone: *He's a man who strikes out with his fists whenever he's angry.* **3** *vi* to swim strongly: *He struck out towards the land.*

strike up 1 *vi, vt sep* to begin to play (a tune *etc*): *The band struck up (with) 'The Red Flag'.* **2** *vt fus* to begin (a friendship, conversation *etc*): *He struck up an acquaintance with a girl on the train.*

string along (*old sl*) **1** *vi* (*with* **with**) to be a girl-friend/boy-friend/companion to: *She has been stringing along with him for years.* **2** *vt oblig sep* to keep (a person) attached to oneself without being seriously committed to him/her: *You're just stringing me along till you find a girl you like better.*

string out *vt sep* (*especially in passive*) to spread or stretch into a long line: *The runners were strung out along the course.*

strip down *vt sep* **1** to remove *eg* wallpaper, paint *etc* from (walls, doors *etc*): *The woodwork should be* stripped down. *Strip the doors down before you put the new paint on.* **2** to remove parts from (an engine *etc*) in order to repair or clean it: *He stripped the engine down and then couldn't put it together again.*

strip off *vi, vt sep* to remove (clothes or a covering) from a thing or person: *He stripped (his clothes) off and had a shower. The doctor stripped his bandage off.*

struggle along *vi (inf)* to have only just enough money to live: *They managed to struggle along somehow.*

stub out *vt sep* to extinguish (a cigarette or cigar) by pressing it against a hard surface: *He stubbed out his cigarette in the ashtray.*

stuff up *vt sep* to block: *He stuffed the hole up with some newspaper. They don't use the fireplace and so they've stuffed up the chimney. I've got a cold and my nose is stuffed up.*

stumble across/on *vt fus* to find (something) by chance: *I stumbled across this book today in a shop. When writing a biography of Napoleon she stumbled across hitherto unknown facts.*

stump up *vi, vt fus (inf)* to pay (a sum of money), often unwillingly: *We all stumped up $10 for his present. We're always being asked to stump up.*

suck up *vi (inf derog) (often with* to*)* to try to gain a person's favour by flattery *etc*: *He's just trying to suck up (to you).*

sum up *vi, vt sep* to give the main or important points of (a discussion *etc*): *He summed up the various arguments against the proposal.*

swab down *vt sep* to wash (a deck): *The sailors were swabbing down the deck.*

swallow up *vt sep (fig)* to swallow completely: *She was swallowed up by the crowd. His wife's clothes bills swallowed up his wages.*

swan around/off *vi (inf derog)* to go travelling in a leisurely and rather irresponsible way: *He swans around doing nothing while his wife works. His job seems to allow him to go swanning off to Italy from time to time.*

swarm up *vt fus* to climb (a tree, wall *etc*) using arms and legs: *The sailors swarmed up the rigging.*

swear in *vt sep* to introduce (a person) into a post or office formally, by making him swear an oath: *The new Governor is being sworn in next week. They swore the jury in yesterday.*

swear to *vt fus* to make a solemn statement, with an oath, about (something): *I'll swear to the truth of what he said. I think he was here this morning, but I wouldn't like to swear to it.*

sweat out *vt sep* to rid oneself of (*eg* a cold) by sweating: *He tried to sweat his cold out by taking aspirins.*

sweep out *vt sep* to sweep (a room *etc*) thoroughly; to clean by sweeping: *The cleaner sweeps the classroom out every evening.*

sweep up *vt sep* to gather or remove (dirt *etc*) by sweeping: *She swept up the crumbs/mess.*

swell out *vi, vt sep* to (cause to) bulge: *The sails swelled out. Her cheeks swelled out. The wind swelled the sails out.*

swell up *vi* (of a part of the body) to swell: *The tooth-ache made her face swell up. Her ankles have swollen up.*

swill out *vt sep* to rinse: *She poured away the dirty water and then swilled the bowl out with fresh water.*

swing to *vi, vt oblig sep* to close: *The gate swung to. Will you swing the gate to?*

switch on, off *vi, vt sep* to put or turn on or off (an electric current/light *etc*): *He switched on the light. You should always switch off the electricity before going on holiday. O.K. switch on now.*

switch over *vi, vt sep* to (cause to) change: *We're switching over to North Sea gas. When are they switching them over?*

swot up *vi, vt sep* (*inf*) to memorize (a subject *etc*), especially for an examination: *I must swot up my history dates/French irregular verbs. I'll have to swot up for my exam.*

T

tack on *vt sep (inf: sometimes derog: sometimes with* **to** *)* to add (something) to (the end of) something: *That last speech in the play doesn't seem to have any purpose — it has just been tacked on at the end to please the producer.*

tag along *vi (inf: sometimes derog: often with* **behind** *or* **with***)* to follow or go (with someone), often when one is not wanted: *We never get away from him — everywhere we go, he insists on tagging along (with us)!*

tag on 1 *vt sep (usually with* **at** *or* **to***)* to attach (something) to something: *These comments weren't part of his speech — he just tagged them on at the end.* **2** *vi (often with* **to***)* to follow (someone) closely: *The child always tags on to his elder brother.*

tail off *vi* **1** to become fewer, smaller or weaker (at the end): *A lot of people came to see the exhibition when it opened, but the crowds tailed off after a couple of weeks. His interest tailed off towards the end of the film.* **2** *(also* **tail away***)* (of voices *etc*) to become quieter or silent: *He realized what he was saying was nonsense, and his voice tailed off into silence. He tailed off when the headmaster entered the room. His voice tailed away into silence.*

take after *vt fus* to be like (someone, especially a parent or relation) in appearance or character: *She takes after her father.*

take back 1 *vt oblig sep* to make (someone) remember or think about (something): *Meeting my old friends took me back to my childhood.* **2** *vt sep* to admit that what has been said is not true; to retract (something that has been said): *Take back what you said about my sister!*

take down *vt sep* to make a note or record of: *He took down her name and address. He took down the details* *in a note book.*

take in *vt sep* **1** to include: *Greater London takes in the county of Middlesex.* **2** to give (someone) shelter: *He had nowhere to go, so I took him in.* **3** to understand and remember: *I didn't take in what he said.* **4** to make (clothes) smaller: *I lost a lot of weight, so I had to take all my clothes in.* **5** to deceive or cheat: *I was told the picture was very valuable, but I soon found out I'd been taken in. He took me in with his story.*

take off 1 *vt sep* to remove (clothes *etc*): *He took off his coat/bandage/mask. I don't know how much this costs — someone has taken the price-tag off.* **2** *vi* (of an aircraft) to leave the ground: *The plane took off for Rome.* **3** *vt oblig sep* not to work during (a period of time): *I'm taking tomorrow morning off.* **4** *vt sep (inf)* to imitate someone (often unkindly): *He used to take off his teacher to make his friends laugh.*

take on 1 *vt sep* to agree to do (work *etc*); to undertake: *He took on the job.* **2** *vt sep* to begin to employ: *They are taking on eighty more men at the factory. They will take more on next year.* **3** *vt sep (with* at*)* to challenge (someone) to a game *etc*: *I'll take you on at tennis.* **4** *vt sep* to get; to assume: *When we learnt all about the poet, his writing took on a completely new meaning.* **5** *vt sep* to allow (passengers) to get on or in: *The bus only stops here to take on passengers — you can't get off here.* **6** *vi (inf)* to be upset: *Don't take on so!*

take over 1 *vi, vt sep* to take control (of): *He has taken the business over.* **2** *vi, vt sep (often with* from*)* to do (something) after someone else stops doing it: *He drove as far as Paris, then I took over (from him). He retired last year, and I took over his job.*

take to *vt fus* **1** to find acceptable or pleasing: *I soon took to her children/idea.* **2** to begin to do (something) regularly: *He took to smoking a pipe.*

take up *vt sep* **1** to use or occupy (space, time *etc*): *I won't take up much of your time. His clothes took up most of the wardrobe.* **2** to begin doing, playing *etc*: *He has* *taken up teaching.* **3** to shorten (clothes): *My skirts were too long, so I had them taken up.* **4** *(old)* to lift or raise; to pick up: *He took up the book.*

take up with *vt fus (inf)* to become friendly with; to associate with: *She has taken up with some very strange people.*

talk back *vi (often with to)* to answer rudely: *Don't talk back (to me)!*

talk down to *vt fus* to speak to (someone) as if he/she is much less important, clever *etc*: *Now that she is at university, she talks down to all her relatives. Children dislike being talked down to.*

talk over *vt sep* to discuss: *We talked over the whole idea. We must talk it over.*

talk round **1** *vt usually sep* to persuade: *I managed to talk her round.* **2** *vt fus* to talk about (something) for a long time without reaching the most important point: *We did not come to a decision about who should get the job although we talked round it for hours.*

tangle with *vt fus (inf)* to become involved in a quarrel or struggle with (a person *etc*): *I tangled with him over politics. I wouldn't like to tangle with a lion.*

tart up *vt sep (sl: often derog)* to make (a person, thing *etc*) more attractive, especially in a showy or tasteless way: *She was tarting herself up in front of the mirror. Their house was nicer before it was tarted up.*

team up *vi (usually with with)* to join with another person in order to do something together: *They decided to team up. They teamed up with another family to rent a house for the summer.*

tear at *vt fus* to pull violently or attack with tearing movements: *The animal's claws tore at his body.*

tear up *vt sep* **1** to remove (something) from a fixed position by violence: *The wind tore up several trees.* **2** to tear into pieces: *She tore up the letter.*

tee up *vi* to tee a golf ball: *He teed up for the first hole.*

tell off *vt sep (inf)* to scold: *The teacher used to tell me off for not doing my homework.*

tell on *vt fus* **1** (*also* **tell upon**: *formal*) to have a bad effect on: *Smoking is telling on his health. The strain of looking after her invalid mother is obviously telling upon her.* **2** (*inf*) to give information about (a person, usually if they are doing something wrong): *I'm late for work — don't tell on me!*

thaw out *vi, vt sep* **1** (of frozen food *etc*) to make or become unfrozen: *We thawed out the frozen meat.* (*fig inf*) *He tried to thaw out in front of the fire.* **2** (*fig inf*) to make or become friendly, less severe *etc*: *A couple of sherries will thaw out the guests and get them chatting to each other.*

thin out *vi, vt sep* to make or become less dense or crowded: *The trees thinned out near the river. I must thin out the turnips — they are much too close together.*

think of *vt fus* **1** to remember to do (something); to keep in one's mind; to consider: *He has a lot of things to think of before he leaves. You think of everything* (= You remember and do everything that needs to be done). *Have you thought of the cost involved?* **2** (with **can** or **could** *in neg*) to remember: *I couldn't think of her name when I met her at the party.* **3** (with **would, should, not, never** *etc*) to be willing to do (something): *I would never think of being rude to her. He couldn't think of leaving her. Such a thing is not to be thought of.* **4** to have a particular idea; to suggest: *That's a brilliant idea. I wonder why no-one thought of it before. I can't think of any way of doing this more efficiently.*

think out *vt sep* to plan; to work out in the mind: *He thought out the whole operation.*

think over *vt sep* to think about (something) carefully; to consider all aspects (of an action, decision *etc*): *He thought it over, and decided not to go.*

think up *vt sep* to invent; to devise: *He thought up a new process.*

thrash out *vt sep* to discuss (a problem *etc*) thoroughly and solve it: *They thrashed it out between them, and finally came to an agreement.*

throw about/around *vt sep* to throw in(to) various places; to scatter: *He threw his paper about. (fig) He throws his money around on expensive luxuries.*

throw away *vt sep* **1** to get rid of: *He always throws away his old clothes.* **2** to lose through lack of care, concern etc: *Don't throw your chance of promotion away by being careless.*

throw in *vt sep (inf)* to include or add as a gift or as part of a bargain: *When I bought his car he threw in the radio and a box of tools. (fig) He threw in a rude remark.*

throw off *vt sep* **1** to get rid of: *She finally managed to throw off her cold. They were following us but we threw them off.* **2** to take off very quickly: *He threw off his coat and sat down.*

throw on *vt sep* to put on (clothes *etc*) very quickly: *He threw on a jacket and ran after her.*

throw out *vt sep* **1** *(inf)* to get rid of by throwing or by force: *He was thrown out of the meeting. (fig) The committee threw out the proposal.* **2** to say something casually or as an offer: *He threw out a remark/a challenge.* **3** to cause to become inaccurate: *This new factor has thrown out all my previous calculations.* **4** to cause to stick out: *He threw out his chest and sang.*

throw over *vt sep (fig inf)* to leave, abandon (a girlfriend, boyfriend *etc*): *She threw him over for someone with more money.*

throw together *vt sep* **1** to bring (people) together (by chance): *They were thrown together by their interest in skiing. She tries to throw those two young people together — she wants them to marry.* **2** *(inf)* to put together in a hurry: *She threw a meal together. She threw her clothes together and put them in a suitcase.*

throw up 1 *vi (sl)* to vomit: *She had too much to eat, and threw up on the way home.* **2** *vt sep (inf)* to give up or abandon: *He threw up his job.* **3** *vt sep (often derog)* to build hurriedly: *They threw up a temporary building.*

thrust on/*(formal)* upon *vt sep* to bring (something or someone) forcibly to someone's notice, into someone's company *etc*: *He thrust $100 on me. She is always thrusting herself on other people. (fig) Fame was thrust upon him.*

tick off *vt sep* **1** to put a tick beside an item or name on a list *etc*: *She ticked each item off on the list as they put it in the van.* **2** to scold: *I was ticked off by her for shouting in the street. He ticked her off for being rude.*

tick over *vi* to run quietly and smoothly at a gentle pace: *The car's engine is ticking over. Our sales are ticking over nicely at the moment.*

tie in/up *vi* (*fig: often with* **with**) to be linked or joined (logically): *This doesn't tie in (with what he said before). These statements don't tie up.*

tinker about/around *vi* to fiddle, or work in an unskilled way (with machinery *etc*): *He enjoys tinkering about/around (with car engines).*

tip off *vt sep* (*inf*) to give information or a hint to; to warn: *He tipped me off about her arrival.*

tip over *vi, vt sep* to knock or fall over; to overturn: *He tipped the lamp over. She put the jug on the edge of the table and it tipped over.*

tire out *vt sep* to tire or exhaust completely: *The hard work tired her out.*

tone down *vi, vt sep* to make or become softer, less harsh *etc*: *The bright colour of the bricks will soon tone down. He toned down some of his criticisms.*

tone up *vt sep* to give strength to; to put in good condition: *The exercise toned up his muscles.*

top up *vt sep* to fill (a cup *etc* that has been partly emptied) to the top: *Let me top up your glass/drink. I'm going to top up the petrol tank. Will you top it up?*

toss off *vt sep* (*inf*) **1** to drink quickly: *He tossed off a pint of beer.* **2** to produce quickly and easily: *He tossed off a few verses of poetry.*

toss up *vi* (*inf*) to toss a coin to decide a matter: *We tossed up (to decide) whether to go to the play or the ballet.*

tot up *vt sep* (*inf*) to add up: *He totted up the figures on the bill. Could you tot up the cost of the meal and let* *me know how much I owe you? If you write down the figures I'll tot them up.*

total up *vi, vt sep* to add up: *He totalled up (the amount he had sold) at the end of the week.*

touch down *vi* **1** (of aircraft) to land: *The plane should touch down at 2 o'clock.* **2** in rugby football, to put the ball on the ground behind the opposite team's goal line.

touch off *vt sep* to make (something) explode: *A spark touched off the gunpowder. (fig) His remark touched off an argument.*

touch on *vt fus* to speak of (a subject) casually; to mention: *He spoke about social conditions, touching on housing and education.*

touch up *vt sep* to improve (*eg* paintwork, a photograph *etc*) by small touches: *He took a brush and touched up the paintwork. The photograph had been touched up.*

track down *vt sep* to pursue or search for (someone or something) until it is caught or found: *I managed to track down an old copy of the book.*

trade in *vt sep* to give (something) as part-payment for something else: *We decided to trade in our old car and get a new one.*

trade on/(*formal*) **upon** *vt fus* (*derog*) to take usually unfair advantage of: *He traded on her kindness.*

trespass on/**upon** *vt fus* (*formal*) to intrude into (a person's time, privacy *etc*): *I don't want to trespass on your time.*

trifle with *vt fus* (*formal*) to act towards (someone or their feelings) without enough respect: *Don't trifle with me! I won't be trifled with. He was trifling with her affections.*

trip up *vi, vt sep* **1** (*also* **trip over**) to (cause to) catch one's foot and stumble or fall: *He tripped up on the carpet. She tripped him up with her foot.* **2** (*fig inf*) to (cause to) make mistakes: *He tripped her up with a difficult question. She spoke well but kept tripping up over foreign words.*

trot out *vt sep (inf derog)* to bring out (usually to show to someone): *He is always trotting out the same excuses for being late.*

trump up *vt sep (inf derog)* to invent or make up (false evidence, accusations *etc*): *He said that the police had trumped up a charge against him.*

try on *vt sep* **1** to put on (clothes *etc*) to see if they fit: *She tried on a new hat. I've bought a dress but I haven't tried it on yet.* **2** *(inf) (usually with* it*)* to attempt to do (something); to indulge in (a certain kind of behaviour *etc*) in order to see whether it will be allowed: *Take no notice of the child's behaviour — he's just trying it on.*

try out *vt sep* to test (something) by using it: *He tried out the bicycle. We are trying out new teaching methods. I think I'd like that washing-machine but I'd like to try it out before I buy it.*

tuck in 1 *vt sep* to gather bedclothes *etc* closely round (someone) especially a child: *I said goodnight and tucked him in.* **2** *vi (inf)* to eat greedily or with enjoyment: *They sat down to breakfast and started to tuck in straight away.*

tuck into *vt fus (inf)* to eat eagerly: *He tucked into his tea.*

tuck up *vt sep* to tuck in: *It's late. You should be tucked up in bed.*

tune in *vi, vt sep (often with* to*)* to tune a radio (to a particular station or programme): *We usually tune (the radio) in to the news.*

tune up *vi* (of an orchestra *etc*) to tune instruments: *The orchestra stopped tuning up just before the conductor came on stage.*

turn away *vi, vt sep* to move or send away: *He turned away in disgust. The police turned away the crowds. The police turned them away.*

turn back *vi, vt sep* to (cause to) go back in the opposite direction: *He got tired and turned back. The travellers were turned back at the frontier. The police turned them back.*

turn down *vt sep* **1** to say 'no' to; to refuse: *He turned* *down her offer/request.* **2** to reduce (the level of light, noise *etc*) produced by (something): *Please turn down (the volume on) the radio — it's far too loud! The lights in the auditorium were turned down before the concert performance.*

turn in *(inf)* **1** *vi* to go to bed: *I usually turn in at about 11 o'clock.* **2** *vt sep* to hand over (a person or thing) to people in authority: *They turned the escaped prisoner in to the police.*

turn off *vt sep* **1** to cause (water, electricity *etc*) to stop flowing: *I've turned off the water/the gas.* **2** to turn (a tap, switch *etc*) so that something stops: *I turned off the tap.* **3** to cause (something) to stop working by switching it off: *He turned off the light/the oven.* **4** *(sl)* to create feelings of dislike, repulsion, disgust *etc* in (someone): *People with loud voices turn me off. I was turned off by the callous treatment of her family.*

turn on 1 *vt sep* to make (water, electric current *etc*) flow: *I've turned on the water/the electricity.* **2** *vt sep* to turn (a tap, switch *etc*) so that something works: *I turned on the tap.* **3** *vt sep* to cause (something) to work by switching it on: *He turned on the radio.* **4** *vt sep* to create feelings of excitement, interest, lust, pleasure *etc* in (someone): *Music really turns me on.* **5** *vt fus* to attack: *The dog turned on him.*

turn out 1 *vt oblig sep* to send away; to make (someone) leave: *His parents threatened to turn him out (= make him leave home) if he ever got into trouble with the police.* **2** *vt sep* to make or produce: *The factory turns out ten finished articles an hour. (fig) The school turns out well-behaved young women.* **3** *vt sep* to empty or clear: *I turned out the cupboard.* **4** *vi* (of a crowd) to come out; to get together for a (public) meeting, celebration *etc*: *A large crowd turned out to see the procession.* **5** *vt sep* to turn off: *Turn out the light.* **6** *vi* to happen or prove to be: *He turned out to be right. It turned out that he was right. The weather turned out (to be) fine. You said we shouldn't trust him, and you* *were right, as it turns out.*

turn over *vt sep* **1** *(fig)* to think about: *She turned it over in her mind.* **2** *(often with* **to***)* to give (something) up (to): *He turned the money over to the police.*

turn to *vi* to get down to (hard) work: *She turned to and scrubbed the floor.*

turn up **1** *vi (inf)* to appear or arrive: *He turned up at our house.* **2** *vi (inf)* to be found: *Don't worry — it'll turn up again.* **3** *vt sep* to increase (the level of noise, light *etc*) produced by (something): *Turn up (the volume on) the radio. The lights in the auditorium were turned up again at the end of the concert performance.* **4** *vt sep* to fold up and sew: *to turn up a hem.* **5** *vt sep (inf)* to discover (facts *etc*): *The police have apparently turned up some new evidence.*

U

urge on *vt sep* to drive or try to persuade (a person *etc*) to go on or forwards: *He tried to urge the donkey on. He urged himself on in spite of his weariness.*

usher in *vt sep* **1** to conduct (a person) into a house, room *etc*: *The door was opened and he was ushered in.* **2** *(liter fig)* to introduce or bring (a period, era *etc*) into existence: *The succession of the new emperor ushered in an era of terror.*

V

venture on/upon *vt fus (formal)* to take the risk of starting on: *You should never have ventured on such a journey/enterprise.*

verge on/upon *vt fus (formal)* to be almost but not quite (something): *His behaviour verges on lunacy at times. What he is asking us to do is verging on the impossible.*

visit with *vt fus (Amer)* to go to see (a person or place); to stay in (a place) or with (a person) for a time: *She is visiting with her parents.*

vouch for *vt fus* **1** to say or declare that one is sure that something is fact or truth: *I can vouch for his honesty. Will you vouch for the truth of the statement.* **2** to guarantee the honesty *etc* of (a person): *My friends will vouch for me.*

W

wade in *vi*, **wade into** *vt fus (inf)* to attack (people, a task *etc*) with enthusiasm and without hesitation: *He waded in at her for her clumsiness. He waded into the discussion without thinking. He really waded into the child for lying to him.*

wait up *vi (sometimes with* **for***)* to stay out of bed at night waiting (for someone to come home): *I'll be late, so don't wait up (for me). The parents waited up till their daughter came in.*

wake up **1** *vi, vt sep* to wake: *I have to leave very early in the morning and I'm afraid that I won't wake up in time. Wake up! You're late. Try and wake him up, will you? The baby woke up in the middle of the night.* **2** *vi (inf: often with* **to***)* to become aware (of): *It is time you woke up to the fact that your wife is being unfaithful. Why don't people wake up and realize what is happening?*

walk away with *vt fus (inf)* to win (prizes *etc*) easily: *Of course you'll win — you'll walk away with all the prizes.*

walk off **1** *vi* to walk away: *He walked off down the* road. **2** *vt sep* to get rid of (*eg* a headache) by walking: *He's gone to try to walk off his hangover.*

walk off with *vt fus* (*inf*) **1** to win easily: *He walked off with all the prizes at the school sports.* **2** to steal: *The thieves have walked off with my best silver and china.*

walk out *vi* to leave (a factory *etc*) on strike: *The entire work-force has walked out (on strike) in protest against the new agreement.*

walk out on *vt fus* (*derog*) to abandon: *He's walked out on his wife/responsibilities.*

wall up *vt sep* to shut (a person) up permanently inside a wall, often alive: *Many years ago, people were sometimes sentenced to death by being walled up.*

want for *vt fus* to lack: *She's never wanted for money or possessions. She wants for nothing* (= She has everything she could wish for).

warm up *vi, vt sep* to make or become moderately warm: *Your feet will soon warm up once you get indoors. The room will soon warm up. Have a cup of coffee to warm you up.*

wash out *vt sep* to ruin, prevent *etc,* especially by rain: *Heavy rain washed out twenty football matches today in southern England.*

wash up 1 *vi, vt sep* to wash (dishes *etc*) after a meal: *I'll help you wash up. We've washed the plates up.* **2** *vi* to wash one's hands and face. **3** *vt sep* (*often in passive*) to bring up on to the shore: *The ship was washed up on the rocks. A lot of rubbish has been washed up on the beach.*

waste away *vi* to decay; to lose weight, strength and health *etc*: *He is wasting away because he has a terrible disease.*

watch out *vi* (*often with* **for**) to be careful (of): *Watch out (for the cars)! Watch out! The police are coming!*

watch over *vt fus* (*formal*) to guard or take care of: *The mother bird is watching over her young.*

water down *vt sep* to dilute: *This milk has been watered down.* (*fig*) *He watered down his comments so that they become less offensive. He watered them down.*

wave aside *vt sep* to dismiss (a suggestion *etc*) without paying much attention to it: *"Of course it won't rain!" she said, waving my objection aside.*

wear away *vi, vt sep* to make or become damaged due to use: *The steps have been worn away over the years. The stonework has worn away in places.*

wear down *vt sep* (*fig*) to lessen (someone's resistence): *They gradually wore him down, and finally he changed his mind.*

wear off *vi* (of effects *etc*) to become less or improve: *The effect of the anaesthetic began to wear off. His headache wore off. The pain is wearing off.*

wear out *vi, vt sep* to (cause to) become unfit for further use: *My socks have worn out. I've worn out my socks.*

weed out *vt sep* (*inf*) to remove (things which are unwanted) from a group or collection: *We'll weed out all the unsuitable candidates and then interview the rest.*

weigh in *vi* **1** to find one's weight before a fight, after a horse-race *etc*. **2** (*often with* **with**) to join in a discussion, project with enthusiasm: *She weighed in with a long list of complaints. Mr Smith has weighed in with an offer of help.*

weigh out *vt sep* to measure out by weighing: *He weighed out six kilos of sand into one-kilo bags.*

weigh up *vt sep* to calculate or assess (a probability *etc*): *He weighed up his chances of success. She weighed the situation up and decided she could win easily. She's good at weighing up people.*

whip up *vt sep* **1** to whip: *Whip up the cream, will you? I'm whipping up eggs for the dessert.* **2** (*inf*) to produce or prepare quickly: *I'll whip up a meal in no time.* **3** to cause with effort; to excite or rouse: *You must try to whip up some enthusiasm for the project. I cannot whip up any support.*

whittle away *vt sep*, **whittle away at** *vt fus* (*usually fig*) to cut away gradually; to reduce: *These bills are whittling away at our savings. They have whittled away a fortune.*

whittle down *vt sep (fig)* to cut down gradually: *We've whittled down the list of applicants to a few whom we wish to interview. Can you whittle it down further?*

win over *vt sep* to succeed in gaining the support and sympathy of: *At first he refused to help us but we finally won him over. You will have to win over the whole committee.*

win through *vi (often with* **to***)* to succeed in getting (to a place, the next stage *etc*): *The soldiers won through to the coast despite heavy losses. It will be a struggle, but we'll win through in the end.*

wind down *vi* **1** (of a clock *etc*) to slow down and stop, because its spring has become uncoiled. **2** (of a person) to relax and become free from tension: *It took her several days of her holiday to wind down after the pressures of her work.*

wind up 1 *vt sep* to turn, twist or coil; to make into a ball or coil: *My ball of wool has unravelled — could you wind it up again?* **2** *vt sep* to wind (a clock, watch *etc*): *She wound up the clock and set the alarm.* **3** *vi, vt sep (inf)* to (cause to) end: *The meeting finally wound up at about four o'clock. I think it's time to wind the meeting up.* **4** *vi (inf)* to end up: *He will wind up in jail. We always wind up by going for a drink.*

wipe out *vt sep* **1** to clean the inside of (something) with a cloth *etc*: *Could you wipe out the washhand basin?* **2** *(fig)* to remove; to get rid of: *You must try to wipe out the memory of these terrible events.* **3** to destroy completely: *They wiped out the whole regiment in one battle.*

wipe up *vt sep* to remove by rubbing with a cloth, paper *etc*: *Please wipe up the spilt milk.* **2** *vi, vt sep* to dry (dishes): *It is your turn to wipe up. I've wiped up the dishes.*

work off *vt sep* to get rid of (something unwanted or unpleasant) by taking physical exercise *etc*: *He worked off his anger by running round the garden six times. He tried to work off some of his excess weight by doing* *exercises every day.*

work out 1 *vt sep* to solve or calculate correctly: *I can't work out how many should be left.* **2** *vi, vt sep* to (cause to) happen successfully: *Don't worry — it will all work out in the end.*

work up 1 *vt sep* to excite or rouse gradually: *She worked herself up into a fury. He's worked his mother up into a state of nervous exhaustion.*

write down *vt sep* to record in writing: *She wrote down every word he said. I can't remember what he said — I didn't write it down.*

write in *vi* to write a letter (especially to a newspaper, radio or TV programme *etc*): *Several readers have written in to say that they like our magazine. I think I'll write in to the newspaper and complain about this article. She wrote in for advice on how to grow roses.*

write off *vt sep* **1** to regard as lost forever: *They wrote off the whole amount that had been spent on the new project. We'll have to write off the printing costs of that book or it will never make a profit.* **2** *(inf)* to destroy completely or damage beyond repair: *He wrote his car off in a bad accident.*

write out *vt sep* to copy or record in(to) writing: *You'll have to write the letter out again, more neatly than before. Write this out in your neatest handwriting.*

write up *vt sep* to bring (a record) up to date: *He wrote up the records of the week's takings.*

Z

zip up *vt sep* to fasten (with a zip fastener): *She zipped up her trousers.*

zoom in *vi (usally with on)* to direct a camera (on to an object *etc*) and use a zoom lens to make it appear to come closer: *Film the whole building first, then zoom in on the door.*